Brain-Powered Lessons to Engage All Learners

Author
LaVonna Roth, M.S.Ed.

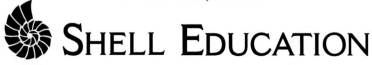
SHELL EDUCATION

Publishing Credits

Robin Erickson, *Production Director*; Lee Aucoin, *Creative Director*;
Timothy J. Bradley, *Illustration Manager*; Emily R. Smith, M.A.Ed., *Editorial Director*;
Jennifer Wilson, *Editor*; Evelyn Garcia, M.A.Ed., *Editor*; Amber Goff, *Editorial Assistant*;
Grace Alba Le, *Designer*; Corinne Burton, M.A.Ed., *Publisher*

Image Credits

All images Shutterstock

Standards

© 2004 Mid-continent Research for Education and Learning (McREL)
© 2007 Teachers of English to Speakers of Other Languages, Inc. (TESOL)
© 2007 Board of Regents of the University of Wisconsin System. World-Class Instructional Design and Assessment (WIDA)
© 2010 National Governors Association Center for Best Practices and Council of Chief State School Officers (CCSS)

Shell Education

5301 Oceanus Drive
Huntington Beach, CA 92649-1030
http://www.shelleducation.com
ISBN 978-1-4258-1180-8
© 2014 Shell Educational Publishing, Inc.

Table of Contents

Table of Contents *(cont.)*

A Letter to You

Dear Educator,

I want to take a moment to thank you for the inspiration that you are! As more mandates fall upon your shoulders and changes are made, I admire your drive, passion, and willingness to keep putting our students first. Every decision we make as educators should come down to one simple question: "Is this decision in the best interest of our students?" This reflects not our opinion, our philosophy, or our own agenda, but simply what is going to make the greatest impact on our students in preparing them for life and career.

As you continue to be the best you can be, I want you to take a few moments each day, look in the mirror, and smile. Come on—I know you can give me a bigger smile than that! Go for the big Cheshire Cat smile with all teeth showing. Why? Because you are sometimes your greatest cheerleader. Now, take that same smile and pass it on to colleagues, students, and parents. Attitude is catching—so let's share the one that puts smiles on others' faces! You will feel better and your day will be better.

Now, tear out this page. Tape it to a place where you will see it every. . . single. . . day. Yep! Tear it out. Tape it to the bathroom mirror, your dashboard, your desk—wherever you are sure to see it. Recite and do the following every single day—no joke:

I am appreciated!

I am amazing!

I am the difference!

From one educator to another, thank you for all you do!

−LaVonna Roth

P.S. Be sure to connect with me on social media! I would love to hear from you on these strategies and lessons.

About the Author

LaVonna Roth, M.S.Ed., is an international author, speaker, and consultant. She has had the privilege of working with teachers on three continents, sharing her passion for education and how the brain learns. Her desire to keep the passion of engaging instructional delivery is evident in her ideas, presentations, workshops, and books.

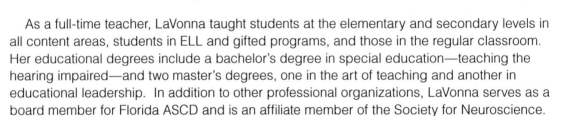

LaVonna has the unique ability to teach some of the more challenging concepts in education and make them simple and doable. Her goal is for teachers to be reenergized, to experience ideas that are practical and applicable, and have a great impact on student achievement because of the effect these strategies have on how the brain learns.

As a full-time teacher, LaVonna taught students at the elementary and secondary levels in all content areas, students in ELL and gifted programs, and those in the regular classroom. Her educational degrees include a bachelor's degree in special education—teaching the hearing impaired—and two master's degrees, one in the art of teaching and another in educational leadership. In addition to other professional organizations, LaVonna serves as a board member for Florida ASCD and is an affiliate member of the Society for Neuroscience.

As an author, she has written a powerful resource notebook, *Brain-Powered Lessons to Engage All Learners*, and is a dynamic and engaging presenter.

When LaVonna isn't traveling and speaking, she relaxes by spending time with her family in the Tampa, Florida area. She is dedicated to putting students first and supporting teachers to be the best they can be.

Acknowledgements

My family
My friends
All educators
Teacher Created Materials staff

I believe we accomplish great things when we surround ourselves with great people and take action. Thank you for all you do!

—LaVonna Roth

The Power of the Brain

"What actually changes in the brain are the strengths of the connections of neurons that are engaged together, moment by moment, in time."

—Dr. Michael Merzenich

The brain is a very powerful organ, one we do not completely understand or know everything about. Yet science reveals more and more to us each day.

As educators, we have a duty to understand how the brain learns so that we can best teach our students. If we do not have an understanding of some of the powerful tools that can help facilitate our teaching and allow us to better target the brain and learning, we lose a lot of time with our students that could be used to serve them better. Plus, the likelihood of doing as much reteaching will lessen.

This is where *Brain-Powered Lessons to Engage All Learners* comes in! The eight strategies included within the lessons are designed around how the brain learns as a foundation. In addition, they are meant to be used as a formative assessment, include higher-order thinking, increase the level of engagement in learning, and support differentiation. For detailed information on each strategy, see pages 12–19.

What Makes the Brain Learn Best

As you explore the strategies in this book, keep the following key ideas in mind.

The content being taught and learned must:

◎ be engaging

◎ be relevant

◎ make sense

◎ make meaning

◎ involve movement

◎ support memory retention

The Power of the Brain *(cont.)*

Be Engaging

In order for students to pay attention, we must engage the brain. This is the overarching theme to the rest of the elements. Too often, students are learning complacently. Just because students are staring at the teacher, with pencil in hand and taking notes, does not mean they are engaged. For example, we know that they are engaged when they answer questions or are interacting with the information independently with a teacher or another student. We don't always know when they are engaged just by looking at them. Sometimes, it's a simple question or observation of what they are doing that helps identify this. Body language can tell us a lot, but do not rely on this as the only point of observation. Many teachers may have not gone into teaching to "entertain," but entertaining is one component of being engaging. As neuroscience research has revealed, it was noted as early as 1762 that the brain does change (neuroplasticity) based on experiences (Doidge 2007). It rewires itself based upon experiences and new situations, creating new neural pathways. "Even simple brain exercises such as presenting oneself with challenging intellectual environments, interacting in social situations, or getting involved in physical activities will boost the general growth of connections" (HOPES 2010, §2). This is fantastic if we are creating an environment and lessons that are positive and planned in a way that fires more neurons that increase accurate learning.

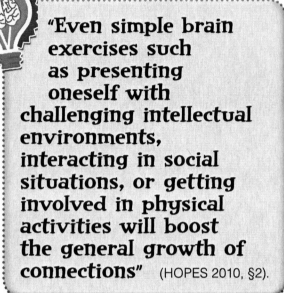

"Even simple brain exercises such as presenting oneself with challenging intellectual environments, interacting in social situations, or getting involved in physical activities will boost the general growth of connections" (HOPES 2010, §2).

The Power of the Brain *(cont.)*

As a reflection for you, think about the following with respect to student engagement:

◎ What are the students doing during the lesson? Are they doing something with the information that shows they are into it? Are they asking questions? Are they answering?

◎ What is their body language showing? Are they slumped, or are they sitting in a more alert position? Are their eyes glazed and half-closed, or are they bright, alert, and paying attention to where their focus should be?

◎ Who is doing most of the talking and thinking? Move away from being the sage on the stage! Let the students be the stars. Share your knowledge with them in increments, but permit them to interact or explore.

◎ What could you turn over to students to have them create a way to remember the content or ask questions they have? What could be done to change up the lessons so they are interacting or standing? Yes, parts of lessons can be taught by having students stand for a minute or so. Before they sit, have them stretch or high-five a few classmates to break up the monotony.

Be Relevant

Why should the brain want to learn and remember something that has no relevance to us? If we want our students to learn information, it is important that we do what we can to make the information relevant. An easy way to achieve this is by bringing in some background knowledge that students have about the topic or making a personal connection. This does not need to take long.

As you will note, the lessons in this book start out with modeling. Modeling allows learners to have an understanding of the strategy and it also takes a moment to bring in what they know and, when possible, to make a personal connection. Consider asking students what they know about a topic and have them offer ideas. Or ask them to reflect on a piece of literature that you read or to ponder a question you have provided. For English language learners, this strategy is particularly effective when they can relate it to something of which they have a foundational concept and can make a connection to what they are learning. The language will come.

Make Sense

Is what you are teaching something that makes sense to students? Do they see the bigger picture or context? If students are making sense of what they are learning, a greater chance of it moving from working memory to long-term memory will increase. Some students can be asked if the idea makes sense and if they clearly understand. If they are able to explain it in their own words, they probably have a good grasp on metacognition and where they are in their learning. Other students may need to be coached to retell you what they just learned.

The Power of the Brain *(cont.)*

Make Meaning

Once students have had an opportunity to make sense of what they are learning, provide an opportunity for them to make meaning. This means that they have a chance to apply what was learned and actually "play" with the skills or concepts. Are they able to complete some tasks or provide questions on their own? Are they ready to take the information to higher levels that demonstrate the depth of understanding? (Refer to Webb's Depth of Knowledge for some additional insight into various levels of making meaning on pages 22–23.) For some students, simply asking a few questions related to what is being taught or having them write a reflection of what was just explained will allow you to check in on their understanding to see where they are before taking their thinking to a higher or a deeper level.

Involve Movement

This one is particularly important because of the plethora of research on movement. Dr. John Ratey wrote the book *Spark*, which documents how student achievement soars based on some changes made to students' physical education program in which students achieved their target heart-rate zone during their physical education time. Movement, particularly exercise, increases brain-derived neurotrophic factors (BDNF) that increase learning and memory (Vaynman, Ying, and Gomez-Pinilla 2004).

Knowing that getting students to achieve their target heart rate zone is not always an option, do what you can. Have students take some brain breaks that heighten their heart rate—even if for just a minute.

Movement has strong retention implications in other ways. Students can create a gesture connected to the lesson concept, or they can stand and move while they make meaning from what they learned. Movement is multisensory, thus, various regions of the brain are activated. When multiple brain pathways are stimulated, they are more likely to enter long-term potentiation from activating episodic and semantic memories.

If you come across a model lesson in this book in which not much movement is shared, or you find your students have been sitting longer than you may wish (you will know because their body language will tell you—unfortunately, we should have had them moving before this point), my challenge to you is to think of what movement you can add to the lesson. It could involve a gesture, a manipulative, or physically getting up and moving. If you are concerned about them calming back down, set your expectations and stick to them. Keep in mind that often when students "go crazy" when permitted to move, it's probably because they *finally* get to move. Try simple techniques to bring students back into focus. "Part of the process of assisting children in developing necessary skills is getting to the root of why they behave as they do" (Harris and Goldberg 2012, xiv).

The Power of the Brain *(cont.)*

Support Memory Retention

If we want our students to retain what we teach them, then it is important that we keep in mind what causes our brains to retain that information.

Key Elements to Memory Retention	Why
Emotions	We can create an episodic memory when we connect emotions to our learning.
Repetition	Repetition increases memory as long as there is engagement involved. Worksheets and drill and kill do not serve long-term memory well.
Patterns/Organization	When our brains take in messages, they begin to file the information by organizing it into categories.
Personal connection	Linking learning to one's self is a powerful brain tool for memory. This, too, can be tied to emotion, making an even stronger connection.
Linking new and prior knowledge	Taking in new information automatically results in connecting past knowledge to what is new.

(Roth 2012)

As you explore the strategies and lessons throughout this book, note how many of them incorporate the keys to memory retention and what engages our students' brains. As you begin to explore the use of these strategies on your own, be sure to keep the framework of those important components.

The bottom line—explore, have fun, and ask your students how they feel about lessons taught. They will tell you if they found the lesson interesting, engaging, and relevant. So get in there, dig in, and have some fun with your students while trying out these strategies and lessons!

It's All About Me
Strategy Overview

Think about the last argument you had with someone. Now, think about your happiest moment. Did the feelings come rushing back and your heart rate speed up, or did an expression cross your face? That is the power of emotion. Science has discovered "that the two structures of the brain that are mainly responsible for long-term memory are located in the emotional area of the brain" (Sousa 2006). Therefore, we need to do what we can to tie content to emotions so that the brain has a greater chance of storing what we teach for the long term.

In addition to emotion, movement and repetition are key to memory retention. In the *It's All About Me* strategy, students take a content area, recall what they already know (or predict what the content entails), and then find ways to make it personal. By making the connection personal, they tie it to a memory they have about someone or something. Be careful that students do not tie it to something personal that was stressful for them, as this can actually hinder the learning. Remember, learning occurs when a positive emotional response is experienced and dopamine, a feel-good chemical, is released. Neuroscience teaches us to incorporate emotions with our cognitive learning because it leads to "the most efficient and effective learning" (Immordino-Yang and Faeth 2010, 74).

Strategy Insight

This strategy takes students through a process that exposes the content to be learned through multiple modalities: visual, auditory, kinesthetic, emotional, and, in some lessons, tactile. The way each lesson is modeled varies depending upon age group, but the core strategy remains consistent throughout all of the lessons. When a movement is learned and we tie it to something personal, we increase the chance of retaining the learning. Movement takes learning from abstract to concrete. It is about students and their connection to the world. Students may copy others, and that is acceptable as long as they can explain the connections and relate it to themselves, personally. Learning to make a personal connection to something is not always easy and usually takes practice.

Teacher Notes

◎ It is important to work with students on difference of opinion here and to respect another person's thoughts and opinions. Students may not understand another student's personal connection, and that is acceptable. You may want to role-play how to respect someone else by teaching them to say something such as "I had not thought of it that way," or "I am glad you found a way to help you understand what we are studying," or "Thank you for sharing with me."

◎ Since this is a personal connection, keep in mind to respect a student's privacy. They may create a way to remember that they do not want to share with you. Encourage them to brainstorm a way that can be shared.

It Takes Two
Strategy Overview

In this strategy, students compare and contrast two topics (e.g., stories, historical figures, types of clouds and shapes) using a T-chart and sticky notes. The goal is for students to analyze each topic and create a chart that represents their thinking. Thereafter, another group of students will evaluate whether it agrees with the original group's thoughts or, if not, if it is going to propose another way to think about the topic. The goal is for students to be able to think at a higher level by justifying either what each sticky note says and where each one is placed or if it qualifies to be on the T-chart at all.

Strategy Insight

Organization and thinking critically are key components in this strategy. Since we organize ideas in our brains systematically and create a neural pathway as more modalities are used, students increase their learning by seeing the information, sorting through what is important, organizing the facts by what is similar and what is different, and adding another level of value through student interaction (Van Tassell 2004). Each of these components plays an integral part in student engagement and retention (Covington 2000). It is another way for students to work with content at a level that is minds-on and hands-on.

Using sticky notes during this activity is important (as opposed to recording the similarities and differences on a sheet) because students' thinking will shift as they discuss and learn more. The sticky notes allow the graphic organizer to become manipulative, and it is a new way for them to see if they agree or disagree with their classmates and adjust accordingly.

Teacher Notes

◎ It is imperative that teachers observe during all stages of the lesson. This provides the feedback we need to determine the next direction of instruction. In addition, it allows an opportunity to guide students in their thinking, as some may struggle with concepts at a higher level. **Note:** Do not guide too much. A large part of learning is struggling through the process with a small amount of frustration but not so much that students give up.

◎ During discussions, students will likely discover that there can be more than one answer. That is where collaboration and cooperation pay off.

◎ For younger students, reconvene as a whole group and model the evaluation steps, using one group's chart.

That's a Wrap!
Strategy Overview

It is important to teach students how to study. Studying can be boring, primarily because it involves repetition. But repetition is one of the keys to memory, as it makes the connections in our brains stronger (Jensen 2005). Willis (2008) further developed this idea by stating that when a greater number of neural connections are activated by the stimulation of practice, an increased number of dendrites grow to strengthen the connections between the neurons.

Strategy Insight

That's a Wrap! is a strategy that helps students learn how to study and how to mix up the repetition with a little fun. Students pull important information, put it into the form of a question, and then write an interview in the form of a script. The interview can be performed in front of the class or other classes, or students can practice at home, using different voices.

Be sure to model. It takes guidance and practice to whittle down information to the key facts or questions. Walk students through the steps to define what is important instead of what is simply a fun fact. Do the facts directly help to answer the essential questions?

As this strategy progresses, encourage students to think about and write questions that are more open-ended than closed-ended. Ainsworth (2003) states that *open-ended* means more than one answer or solution. *Closed-ended* is one answer or solution, often a yes/no response. Open-ended takes more time and more thinking because several factors are taken into consideration; it is not just one simple answer.

If the teacher wants to know if students have moved the learning from working memory to long-term memory, quiz them after 24 hours. If students can recall the information or idea with no advance notification, then the content is making its way into long-term storage. On the same note, this "pop quiz" can be used to check what they remember, and it should not be graded. It is a formative assessment for students to determine what they still need to study.

Teacher Notes

◎ Remember, emotions are a key to increasing memory, along with repetition. As students write the script and rework it, they are repeatedly seeing the information.

◎ Model the cue often used by teachers: Pause when something key is about to be presented. State, "This is important" or "This will be on the test." If information is written on the board, change colors when writing the important fact.

ABC Professors
Strategy Overview

This strategy is best used after students have studied a topic. They become "professors" or "experts" because they have the knowledge base that is necessary to complete a task about the topic.

After students are taught what they need to know, have them begin thinking about the topic. Portions of the strategy are modeled. Then students, with guidance, brainstorm words or phrases about their topic that begin with each letter of the alphabet. The goal is to have a word or phrase for each letter of the alphabet filled in on their *ABC Professor Notes* activity sheet (page 85). This strategy is motivating and can ease the challenging task of asking more inquisitive questions.

Strategy Insight

Although this strategy is meant as a review, it could be used as a formative preassessment to see what students know before a topic is introduced and then used again to see the growth that occurred after teaching the topic. Once students are comfortable with the strategy, they can be given the opportunity to choose their own topic (McCombs 1997).

This strategy can be used as a "sneak peek" to find out what students know, but teachers should watch for the level of frustration. When too much frustration occurs, the stress blockers begin to hinder thinking, and learning declines (Medina 2008). Teachers should challenge students so that their brains seek the pleasure of the intrinsic rewards of learning. According to Csikszentmihalyi (1996), teachers need to keep students in the "flow," a level of challenge that is not too high or low and one that keeps them motivated and engaged, as well.

During the Evaluate/Create component of the strategy, students are challenged to ask questions in alphabetical order and provide a response to the questions their partners ask. Students do not necessarily need to answer the questions. This strategy is to get them thinking and wondering, becoming curious enough to seek answers or speculate about possible answers.

Teacher Notes

◎ Not every box needs to be filled when completing the *ABC Professor Notes* activity sheet. Instead of limiting the number of letters or excluding certain letters, make it a challenge for certain identified students to see how many quality words or phrases they can think of. If it becomes apparent that they have reached a high level of frustration, then ask them which boxes they would like to reasonably eliminate.

◎ If using this as a priming activity, have students record their responses so that they can assess what they used to think, what they now think, and the depth of learning that occurred as they reflect back.

WPH Accordion
Strategy Overview

Think of a mystery story. Who or what is involved? What do you predict will happen? What does happen? These questions make up the *WPH Accordion* strategy. Each of these components plays a key part in motivation, engagement, and memory.

Asking *who* or *what* is involved (*W*) preps our brains to think about the topic. Who or what could be involved in the story, event, experiment, or solution? This question piques our brains' interest because we want to know. The brain likes to learn (Willis 2008).

What do you *predict* (*P*) will happen? Our brains love to predict and to get it right. When our predictions are right, dopamine receptors are activated and our brain experiences that as pleasurable, which increases our reward response (Rock 2009). Emotions come into play, which is important for long-term memory (Jensen 2005). When our predictions are wrong, dopamine levels reduce and the brain works to remember it correctly so it can have the pleasure from dopamine rising (Willis 2008).

What actually *happens (H)*? The brain receives the message whether the prediction is right or not. Our brains use this information for future predictions. Did what we think was going to happen occur?

Strategy Insight

When working with students, it is important to create a culture in which it is okay to be wrong. Often, predictions are wrong; it is how we react that makes a difference. What matters is what we do with that information. If students pull what they know from background knowledge to figure out a mystery component and if they ask questions based on what they know, then that is a start to making good predictions. Teachers should empower students to become aware of what they know and what they are thinking, and that being wrong tells their brains to pay attention to the correct way (Flavell 1979; Willis 2008; Baker 2009).

Students work with topics that have a twist or an unexpected outcome. This allows us to think logically about a solution and also pulls information from the creative side of our brains. Teachers need to encourage students to do their own thinking, ask questions, and work to figure out the result.

Teacher Notes

◎ Provide students the option to draw or write in order to meet the differentiation needs of learners.

◎ You may need more than two sets of the WPH Accordion. If more than two sets are needed, accordion-fold the other half-sheet of paper and tape it to the end of the first accordion. This gives you four sets of W-P-H sections.

Matchmaker
Strategy Overview

The importance of movement and having students get up out of their seats cannot be emphasized enough. Thus, here is another strategy that allows our students to do so. *Matchmaker* also provides students an opportunity to get repeated practice in an environment in which the repetition is guided and correct. This means that when students practice repeatedly, the likelihood of recall increases. A key factor here is that it must be correct practice. When students do this activity with one another, they are getting a chance to see repeated practice with automatic feedback provided about whether they are correct or not.

Strategy Insight

Every student is given an address label to wear. Each label is a vocabulary word, a concept, a formula, etc. On index cards are the matching definitions, illustrations, examples, synonyms, etc.

Students wear the address labels and stand in a circle with the index cards on the floor in the middle. Students hold hands and bend down to pick up an index card with their connected hands. Without letting go, they have to get the card they picked up to the correct person, according to his or her address label. This strategy can be repeated as many times as you wish to help students practice.

Teacher Notes

◎ An alternative to this is for students to not hold hands when they pick up a card. However, energy and engagement increase with the added challenge of holding hands and not letting go.

◎ Be sure to listen in and encourage students to discuss disagreements or to have them respond to a reason why a particular card goes with another card.

Just Say It
Strategy Overview

Working together and hearing thoughts and language are beneficial to all learners, but these things can be especially beneficial to English language learners. *Just Say It* permits students not only to use what they have read, written, or heard but to have a chance to use listening skills for the content as well. A challenge layer to this strategy is having students hold back on a response for a period of time. This allows the one student to say what he or she needs to say before the partner inflicts his or her opinion or factual information upon him or her. It teaches the skill of patience, listening, and being open to others' thoughts at the same time.

Strategy Insight

Students are to respond to their partners, providing feedback and information on a given topic (e.g., a writing prompt, thoughts, an idea). Have students sit facing their partners (sitting at desks is preferable). Identify Partner *A* as the person closest to the front of the room and Partner *B* as the person closest to the back of room. Have Partner *A* start. Partner *A* shares his or her thinking with Partner *B* as Partner *B* only listens for 30 seconds. After 30 seconds, Partner *B* responds to Partner *A*. They then switch roles—Partner *B* shares while *A* listens. Then *A* provides insight or feedback. Students should record (during or at the end), what their partners say for further consideration and use that to write about the topic.

Teacher Notes

◎ You may wish to shorten or lengthen the time each partner has, depending upon the topic and age.

◎ Using a timer, a train whistle, or a bell is a great way to help partners know when to switch, since conversations may get lively or partners may tune out other nearby sounds.

Reverse, Reverse!
Strategy Overview

Reverse, Reverse! is meant to be a challenging strategy. When students are under stress, there will often be not only a chemical but a physical change in the brain. Students must learn the skills to deal with stress, but in a safe and friendly environment. In this strategy, students will practice the speed and fluency of facts, but they will do so under pressure—a pressure that you can adjust or increase, depending upon the topic and age level of your students.

Strategy Insight

Students sit or stand in a circle. They are given a topic and asked to brainstorm what they know about it. One student begins by sharing a fact about the topic. Going clockwise, the next student must quickly say another fact related to the one just stated. If the student pauses more than five seconds or states an incorrect fact, the student that just finished must state the next fact (reversing the direction of participation). One student sits out to judge the facts and make sure rules are followed. Continue until participation stalls. For example, a math activity using this strategy can include counting by threes. The first student says, "3;" the next student says, "6;" the next says, "9." If the following student says, "13," the rotation reverses to the previous student, who must say, "Reverse," and must also say the correct answer, "12." The responses are now going counterclockwise. An example of using this strategy in social studies can include the three branches of government. The first student might say, "Legislative branch;" the second says, "Makes the laws;" the third student says, "Congress;" and the fourth says, "Checks and balances." The judge (student sitting out) can halt the flow to ask how the response relates to a previously said fact. If justified, the round continues. *Reverse, Reverse!* continues until a predetermined amount of clock time or number of times around the circle has been met.

Teacher Notes

◎ It is important to set the stage for students to feel safe when using this strategy. You may wish to take out the reverse portion at first and work on just the speed. Add the extra layer of difficulty for novelty and time-pressured practice.

◎ For younger students, you may choose to not have the next student say, "Reverse," but instead state the correct fact.

How to Use This Book

Lesson Overview

The following lesson components are in each lesson and establish the flow and success of the lessons.

Icons state the brain-powered strategy and one of the four content areas addressed in the book: language arts, mathematics, science, or social studies.

Each lesson revolves around one of the eight **brain-powered strategies** in this book. Be sure to review the description of each strategy found on pages 12–19.

Vocabulary that will be addressed in the lesson is called out in case extra support is needed.

The **procedures** provide step-by-step instructions on how to implement the lessons successfully.

The **standard** indicates the objective for the lesson.

A **materials** list identifies the components of the lesson.

Many lessons contain a **preparation note** that indicates action needed prior to implementing the lessons. Be sure to review these notes to ensure a successful delivery of the lesson.

The **model** section of the lesson provides teachers the opportunity to model what is expected of students and what needs to be accomplished throughout the lesson.

The **apply/analyze** section of the lesson provides students with the opportunity to apply what they are learning as they analyze the content and work toward creating a personal connection.

The **evaluate/create** section of the lesson provides students with the opportunity to think critically about the work of others and then to take ownership of their learning by designing the content in a way that makes sense to them.

How to Use This Book *(cont.)*

Lesson Overview *(cont.)*

Some lessons require **activity cards** to be used. You may wish to laminate the activity cards for added durability. Be sure to read the preparation note in each lesson to prepare the activity cards, when applicable.

Activity sheets are included for lessons that require them. They are to be used either in groups, individually, or just by the teacher. If students are working in groups, encourage them to create a group name to label the activity sheet.

All of the activity sheets and additional teacher resources can be found on the **Digital Resource CD**.

How to Use This Book *(cont.)*

Implementing Higher-Order Thinking in the Lessons

What Is Higher-Order Thinking?

Higher-order thinking occurs on a different level than memorizing facts or telling something back to someone exactly the way it was told (Thomas and Thorne 2009). As educators, it is important to be aware of the level of thinking that students are asked to do. If teachers record the number of questions they ask students on a recall or restate level as well as how many were asked at a higher level, they may be surprised at the imbalance. How do they expect students to think at a higher level if they are not challenged with higher-order questions and problems? Students should be given questions and assignments that require higher-order thinking.

Higher-order thinking also involves critical thinking. If teachers want students to remember facts and think critically, they need to have them be engaged and working with the content at a higher level so that it creates understanding and depth. In addition, higher-order thinking and critical thinking are imperative to 21st century skills. Employers want workers who can problem-solve and work cooperatively to find multiple solutions. The lessons in this resource gradually place more ownership of the learning process in the hands of students as they simultaneously move through higher-order thinking.

Bloom's Taxonomy and Webb's Depth of Knowledge

Throughout the history of education, structures were created to guide teachers in ways to evoke higher-order thinking. Two of the more popular structures are Bloom's Taxonomy and Webb's Depth of Knowledge (DOK).

Benjamin Bloom developed Bloom's Taxonomy as a way to classify educational learning objectives in a hierarchy. In 2001, Lorin Anderson, a former student of Bloom's, worked with some teachers to revise Bloom's original taxonomy by changing the terminology into verbs and switching the top two levels so that *create* (synthesis) is at the top and *evaluate* (evaluation) is just below (Overbaugh and Schultz n.d.).

Norman Webb created Depth of Knowledge in 1997 in order to assist with aligning the depth and complexity of a standard with its assessment. This structure focuses on how the verb is used in the context of what is asked of the student (Webb 2005). DOK correlates with Backwards Planning (Wiggins and McTighe 2005) in that the standards are addressed first and then an assessment that targets the standards is developed or selected.

How to Use This Book *(cont.)*

It is important that teachers instruct students at cognitive levels that meet their needs while challenging them, as well. Whether students are below level, on level, or above level, teachers should use the tools necessary to help them succeed. Using Webb's DOK gives us the tools to look at the end result and tie complexity to the assessment. Bloom's Taxonomy helps to guide depth of assignments and questions. Where the two meet is with the word complexity. Complexity is rigor. Complexity is the changing of levels within Bloom's, and DOK is the amount of depth of thinking that must occur. We want rigor, and thus, we want complexity in our teachings.

Bloom's Taxonomy	Webb's Depth of Knowledge
Knowledge/Remembering The recall of specifics and universals, involving little more than bringing to mind the appropriate material.	**Recall** The recall of a fact, information, or procedure (e.g., What are three critical-skill cues for the overhand throw?).
Comprehension/Understanding The ability to process knowledge on a low level such that the knowledge can be reproduced or communicated without a verbatim repetition.	**Skill/Concept** The use of information, conceptual knowledge, procedures, two or more steps, etc.
Application/Applying The ability to use information in another familiar situation.	**Strategy Thinking** Requires reasoning, developing a plan or sequence of steps; has some complexity; more than one possible answer.
Analysis/Analyzing The ability to break information into parts to explore understandings and relationships.	**Extended Thinking** Requires an investigation as well as time to think and process multiple conditions of the problem or task.
Synthesis and Evaluation/Evaluating and Creating Putting together elements and parts to form a whole and then making value judgements about the method.	

Adapted from Wyoming School Health and Physical Education (2001)

Correlation to the Standards

Shell Education is committed to producing educational materials that are research and standards based. In this effort, we have correlated all of our products to the academic standards of all 50 states, the District of Columbia, the Department of Defense Dependents Schools, and all Canadian provinces.

How to Find Standards Correlations

To print a customized correlation report of this product for your state, visit our website at http://www.shelleducation.com and follow the on-screen directions. If you require assistance in printing correlation reports, please contact our Customer Service department at 1-877-777-3450.

Purpose and Intent of Standards

Legislation mandates that all states adopt academic standards that identify the skills students will learn in kindergarten through grade twelve. Many states also have standards for Pre–K. This same legislation sets requirements to ensure the standards are detailed and comprehensive.

Standards are designed to focus instruction and guide adoption of curricula. Standards are statements that describe the criteria necessary for students to meet specific academic goals. They define the knowledge, skills, and content students should acquire at each level. Standards are also used to develop standardized tests to evaluate students' academic progress. Teachers are required to demonstrate how their lessons meet state standards. State standards are used in the development of all of our products, so educators can be assured they meet the academic requirements of each state.

Common Core State Standards

Many lessons in this book are aligned to the Common Core State Standards (CCSS). The standards support the objectives presented throughout the lessons and are provided on the Digital Resource CD (filename: standards.pdf).

TESOL and WIDA Standards

The lessons in this book promote English language development for English language learners. The standards listed on the Digital Resource CD (filename: standards.pdf) support the language objectives presented throughout the lessons.

Standards Chart

Common Core State Standard	Lesson(s)
Reading: Informational Text.3.6—Distinguish their own point of view from that of the author of a text	Take a Stance p. 99
Reading: Literature.3.1—Ask and answer questions to demonstrate understanding of a text, referring explicitly to the text as the basis for the answers	Find Me a Reference p. 74; Prove It! p. 145
Reading: Literature.3.2—Determine the main idea of a text; recount the key details, and explain how they support the main idea	Mastering the Main Idea p. 62
Math 3.OA.3—Use multiplication and division within 100 to solve word problems in situations involving equal groups, arrays, and measurement quantities, e.g., by using drawings and equations with a symbol for the unknown number to represent the problem	Wise Word Problems p. 127
Math 3.MD.2—Measure and estimate liquid volumes and masses of objects using standard units of grams (g), kilograms (kg), and liters (l). Add, subtract, multiply, or divide to solve one-step word problems involving masses or volumes that are given in the same units, e.g., by using drawings (such as a beaker with a measurement scale) to represent the problem	Mass Wizards p. 86
Math 3.MD.4—Generate measurement data by measuring lengths using rulers marked with halves and fourths of an inch. Show the data by making a line plot, where the horizontal scale is marked off in appropriate units: whole numbers, halves, or quarters	Measurement Mania p. 97
Math 3.MD.5—Recognize area as an attribute of plane figures and understand concepts of area measurement	Tile Equations p. 116
Writing 3.2—Write informative/explanatory texts to examine a topic and convey ideas and information clearly	Concluding Statements p. 122
Writing 3.2.c—Use linking words and phrases (e.g., *also, another, and, more, but*) to connect ideas within categories of information	Missing Links p. 101

Standards Chart *(cont.)*

Common Core State Standard	Lesson(s)
Writing 3.2.d—Provide a concluding statement or section	Concluding Statements p. 122
Writing 3.3—Write narratives to develop real or imagined experiences or events using effective technique, descriptive details, and clear event sequences	Tell Me a Story p. 134
Writing.3.3.a—Establish a situation and introduce a narrator and/or characters; Organize an event sequence that unfolds naturally in a written narrative	Event Sequencing p. 94
Writing 3.3.c—Use temporal words and phrases to signal event order	Missing Links p. 101

McREL Standard	Lesson(s)
Language Arts 5.10—Understands the author's purpose (e.g., to persuade, to inform) or point of view	Getting to the Point (of View) p. 43
Math 1.2—Represents problems situations in a variety of forms (e.g., translates from a diagram to a number or symbolic expression)	Tile Equations p. 116
Math 2.5—Understands the concepts related to fractions (e.g., numerator and denominator, equivalence, relative magnitudes) and decimals (e.g., relative magnitudes)	Pizza Party! p. 35
Math 6.5—Reads and interprets simple bar graphs, pie charts, and line graphs	Data Displays p. 51
Math 6.6—Understands that data come in many different forms and that collecting, organizing, and displaying data can be done in many ways	Data Displays p. 51
Science 1.1—Knows that water exists in the air in different forms (e.g., in clouds and fog as tiny droplets; in rain, snow, and hail) and changes from one form to another through various processes (e.g., freezing, condensation, precipitation, evaporation)	Water: A Case of Multiple Identities p. 71
Science 3.0—Understands the composition and structure of the universe and the Earth's place in it	Stars and Planets: Same or Different? p. 58

Standards Chart *(cont.)*

McREL Standard	Lesson(s)
Science 4.1—Knows that many characteristics of plants and animals are inherited from its parents (e.g., eye color in human beings, fruit or flower color in plants), and other characteristics result from an individual's interactions with the environment (e.g., people's table manners, ability to ride a bicycle)	Family Traits p. 39
Science 10.1—Knows that magnets attract and repel each other and attract certain kinds of other materials (e.g., iron, steel)	Repel or Attract? p. 131
Science 12.4—Uses appropriate tools and simple equipment (e.g., thermometers, magnifiers, microscopes, calculators, graduated cylinders) to gather scientific data and extend the senses	Inquiry Tools p. 90
Social Studies 1.1—Knows the basic elements of maps and globes (e.g., title, legend, cardinal and intermediate directions, scale, grid, principal parallels, meridians, projection)	Mapping Madness p. 29
Social Studies 2.1—Knows major physical and human features of places as they are represented on maps and globes (e.g., shopping areas, fast food restaurants, fire stations, largest cities, rivers, lakes, wetlands, recreation areas, historic sites, land forms, locations of places discussed in history, language arts, science, and other school subjects)	Map Experts p. 77
Social Studies 2.3—Knows the approximate location of major continents, mountain ranges, and bodies of water on Earth	Where Am I? p. 109
Social Studies 3.7—Knows the chronological order of major historical events that are part of the states' history, their significance and the impact on people then and now, and their relationship to the history of the nation	History Buff p. 138
Social Studies 17.2—Knows the major responsibilities of the legislative, executive, and judicial branches of his or her state government	The Power of the Law p. 68

Standards Chart *(cont.)*

TESOL and WIDA Standard	Lesson(s)
English language learners **communicate** for **social**, **intercultural**, and **instructional** purposes within the school setting	All Lessons
English language learners **communicate** information, ideas, and concepts necessary for academic success in the area of **language arts**	All Lessons

Content Area Correlations Chart

Content Area	Lessons
Reading	Getting to the Point (of View) p. 43; Mastering the Main Idea p. 62; Find Me a Reference p. 74; Prove It! p. 145
Writing	Event Sequencing p. 94; Take a Stance p. 99; Missing Links p. 101; Concluding Statements p. 122; Tell Me a Story p. 134
Math	Pizza Party! p. 35; Data Displays p. 51; Mass Wizards p. 86; Measurement Mania p. 97; Tile Equations p. 116; Wise Word Problems p. 127
Social Studies	Mapping Madness p. 29; The Power of the Law p. 68; Map Experts p. 77; Where Am I? p. 109; History Buff p. 138
Science	Family Traits p. 39; Stars and Planets: Same or Different? p. 58; Water: A Case of Multiple Identities p. 71; Inquiry Tools p. 90; Repel or Attract? p. 131

Mapping Madness

Brain-Powered Strategy	Standard
It's All About Me	Knows the basic elements of maps and globes

Vocabulary Words

- compass
- grid
- hemisphere
- key
- legend
- scale

Materials

- *Map Notes* (page 31)
- *Geography Toolkit Cards* (pages 32–33)
- *Our Illustrations* (page 34)
- various maps (e.g., park, state, town, amusement park, zoo)
- globe
- four index cards
- chart paper and markers

Preparation Note: Prior to the lesson, collect at least four different maps for students to study, including at least one globe. Additionally, label each index card with the numbers 1–4. Last, make three copies of the *Our Illustrations* activity sheet (page 34) for each student, and cut apart the *Geography Toolkit Cards* (pages 32–33).

Procedures

Model

1. Display a variety of different types of maps at stations around the classroom. Place one numbered index card next to each map. Distribute copies of the *Map Notes* activity sheet (page 31) to students. Have students circulate around the classroom and take notes on their activity sheets about the unique features of each map displayed. Also, have them observe and record similarities between the maps.

2. After students have had a chance to review the maps, hold a class discussion about the differences they observed.

3. Ask students to note the similarities among the maps. Guide them to identify salient features such as the *legend, scale, key, compass, grid*, and *hemispheres*. Discuss the meanings of these words, and locate these features on each map.

4. Explain the *It's All About Me* strategy to students. (For detailed information on this strategy, see page 12.) Show an example of a movement you associate with the word *compass*, and conduct a think-aloud to illustrate how you came up with your movement.

Mapping Madness *(cont.)*

Apply/Analyze

5. Ask students to think about a movement that would remind them of the meaning of the word *compass*. On the count of three, have each student turn to his or her partner and demonstrate his or her personal movement for the word.

6. Demonstrate how to create a drawing that connects the word *compass* to its meaning on the board.

7. Arrange desks into six stations and place one card from the *Geography Toolkit Cards* at each station. Divide students equally among the stations, and assign each student a partner. Working in pairs, have students use the *It's All About Me* strategy to develop a movement and illustration to help them connect the word to its meaning.

8. Distribute a sheet of chart paper to each group. Ask students at each station to record their illustrations on the sheet of chart paper. Instruct students to write the word in pencil on the back of the paper, and to remove the Geography Toolkit Card assigned to them.

Evaluate/Create

9. Once each group has compiled its illustrations on the chart paper, have students rotate from station to station, discussing the illustrations and answering the following questions:

- What is the word?

- How is the meaning of the word captured in your classmates' illustrations?

- Is there anything you would add or change to capture the meaning in a different way or make it more personally meaningful?

10. Distribute three copies of the *Our Illustrations* activity sheet to each student. Ask each student to work with a partner to choose one illustration from the chart paper for each word. Then, have each student draw and describe it in the left box of his or her activity sheet.

11. Have each student work independently to create and describe his or her personal drawing on the right side of the activity sheet. Students may choose to combine two or more drawings to create their own illustrations.

12. Ask each student to create a new movement for the new words. Then, have them share their new movements with a partner.

Name: _____   Date: _____

Map Notes

Directions: As you visit each station, record the title of the map at the top of the box. Note the unique features of the map. Also, observe and record similarities between the maps.

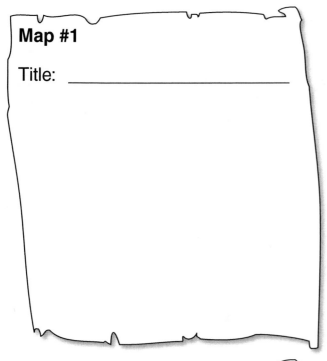

Map #1

Title: _____

Map #2

Title: _____

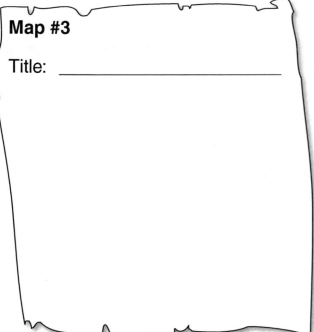

Map #3

Title: _____

Map #4

Title: _____

Geography Toolkit Cards

Teacher Directions: Cut apart the cards below. Place one card at each station.

legend

compass

scale

Geography Toolkit Cards *(cont.)*

hemisphere

grid

key

Name: _____   Date: _____

Our Illustrations

Directions: Write the provided word at each station and draw a picture of an illustration created by one of your classmates. Below each picture, describe the drawing, using words. Then, draw and describe your own illustration in the box in the column on the right.

Group Illustrations	My Illustrations
Word:	
_____	_____
_____	_____
Word:	
_____	_____
_____	_____

Pizza Party!

Brain-Powered Strategy	**Standard**
It's All About Me	Understands the concepts related to fractions

Vocabulary Words

- denominator
- fraction
- numerator
- whole

Materials

- *Pizza Party* (page 37)
- *Pizza Fraction Cards* (page 38)
- *Our Illustrations* (page 34)
- uncut pizza (real or pretend)
- pizza cutter or scissors
- red and yellow markers
- chart paper and markers

Preparation Note: If not using a real pizza, prior to the lesson, create a large pretend pizza out of construction paper. Make two copies of the *Our Illustrations* activity sheet (page 34) for each student. Last cut apart the *Pizza Fraction Cards* (page 38).

Procedures

Model

1. Show students a whole, uncut pizza (real or pretend) and ask them, "How many of you like pizza?" Discuss how you want to cut the pizza into two equal-sized pieces, asking for student input. Demonstrate how to cut it directly down the middle in order to ensure that the pieces are the same size.

2. Write the fraction $\frac{1}{2}$ on the board and discuss the meaning of the word *fraction*. Explain how the number on the top is called the *numerator* and the number on the bottom is the *denominator*. Tell students that when the numerator and the denominator are the same, it is called a *whole*.

3. Demonstrate how to cut the pizza into fourths, writing the fractions $\frac{1}{4}$, $\frac{2}{4}$, $\frac{3}{4}$, and $\frac{4}{4}$ on the board. Review how these fractions correspond to the pizza. Restate the terms *numerator, denominator, fraction*, and *whole* as you discuss the fractions with students.

4. Distribute copies of the *Pizza Party* activity sheet (page 37) to students, and have students divide the pizza by coloring the pieces they want to eat red and the pieces they plan to share with a friend yellow. Have them write the fraction that corresponds to the number of pieces they plan to eat at the bottom of the activity sheet.

Pizza Party! *(cont.)*

5. Explain the *It's All About Me* strategy to students. (For detailed information on this strategy, see page 12.) Tell students that they are going to create a movement to help them remember the meaning of the terms *fraction*, *whole*, *numerator*, and *denominator*. Think aloud while you demonstrate a movement that you created to remember the meaning of the word *denominator*.

6. Have students turn to a partner and take turns sharing their own think-alouds and corresponding movements for the word *denominator*.

7. Model a drawing that either captures your movement for the word *denominator* or represents the literal meaning of the word.

Apply/Analyze

8. Arrange the desks into four stations and divide students evenly among them. At each station, place a different card from the *Pizza Fraction Cards* activity sheet. Have students use the *It's All About Me* strategy to create a movement and illustration for the word at their station.

9. Distribute a sheet of chart paper to each group. Ask students at each station to record their illustrations on the sheet of chart paper. Instruct students to write the word on the back of the paper in pencil, and to remove the *Pizza Fraction Card* assigned to them.

Evaluate/Create

10. Instruct students to rotate from station to station so they can review the other groups' illustrations. Ask students to consider the following questions as they examine the chart paper at each station:

- What word do you think these illustrations represent?

- How did your classmates capture the meaning of the word in their illustrations?

- Is there anything you would add or change to make the connection between the illustration and the word more meaningful to you?

11. Distribute copies of the *Our Illustrations* activity sheet (page 34) to students. Ask each student to work with a partner to choose one illustration from the chart paper for each word. Then, have each student draw and describe it in the left box of his or her activity sheet.

12. Working independently, have students create and describe their own illustrations in the box on the right side of the activity sheet. If they choose, they can combine illustrations from their classmates.

13. Ask students to create a new movement for each word. Then, have them share their new movements with a partner.

Name: _____   Date: _____

Pizza Party

Directions: Color the pieces of pizza that you want to eat red. Color those that you plan to share with your friend yellow.

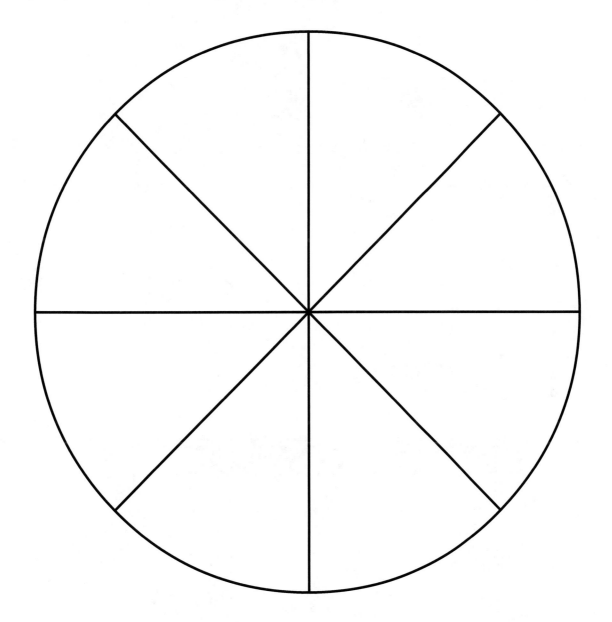

What fraction of the pizza do you plan to eat? Write the number of red pieces that you plan to eat above the line and the total number of pieces in the entire pizza below the line

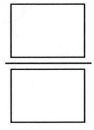

Pizza Fraction Cards

Teacher Directions: Cut apart the cards below. Place one at each station.

fraction $\frac{3}{4}$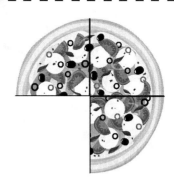

numerator $\frac{1}{4}$

denominator $\frac{3}{4}$

whole $\frac{4}{4}$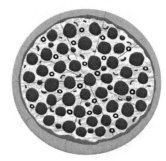

Family Traits

Brain-Powered Strategy

It's All About Me

Standard

Knows that many characteristics of plants and animals are inherited from its parents, and other characteristics result from an individual's interactions with the environment

Vocabulary Words

- acquired traits
- hereditary
- inherited traits
- parent

Materials

- *Inherited Traits* (page 41)
- *Hereditary Trait Cards* (page 42)
- *Our Illustrations* (page 34)
- picture of a set of parents and their child(ren)
- pictures of parent flowering plants and young flowering plants with the same color flowers
- picture of yourself as a child with your parents (*optional*)
- student or generic family photographs
- chart paper and markers

Preparation Note: Prior to the lesson, ask each student to bring in color photographs of his or her parents. Consider modifying the *Inherited Traits* activity sheet (page 41) by using generic family photographs instead of personal ones if you have students who are adopted or do not know their biological family members. Make two copies of the *Our Illustrations* activity sheet (page 34) for each student. Last, cut apart the *Hereditary Trait Cards* (page 42).

Procedures

Model

1. Display a picture of a set of parents and their child(ren) on the board or projector. Discuss the visual similarities (e.g., eye color, hair texture, eye shape). Change the pictures to show a parent flowering plant and a young flowering plant, and discuss the similarities.

2. Explain that some characteristics are *hereditary*, while others are *acquired*. Provide examples of *hereditary* (e.g., eye color) and *acquired* (e.g., ability to ride a bike) traits.

Family Traits *(cont.)*

3. If possible, display a picture of yourself as a child with your parents. Discuss which traits you inherited from each parent. Ask students to get out their family photographs. Distribute a copy of the *Inherited Traits* activity sheet to each student. Have students mark the traits that they inherited from their parents.

4. Explain the *It's All About Me* strategy to students. (For detailed information on this strategy, see page 12.) Explain to students that they will create movements to help them remember the meaning of the terms *parent*, *hereditary*, *inherited trait*, and *acquired trait*. Think aloud while you demonstrate how to create a movement for the word *hereditary*. Draw a picture that represents the meaning of the word and explain your drawing to the class.

Apply/Analyze

5. Arrange the desks into four stations, and divide students evenly among them. Place one card from the *Hereditary Trait Cards* at each station. Working in pairs, have students use the *It's All About Me* strategy to create a movement and an illustration for the word on the card.

6. Distribute a sheet of chart paper to each group. Ask students at each station to record their illustrations on a sheet of chart paper. Instruct students to write the word on the back of the paper in pencil, and remove the *Hereditary Trait Card* assigned to them.

Evaluate/Create

7. Have students rotate from station to station so that they can review the other groups' illustrations. Ask students to consider the following questions as they examine the chart paper at each station:

   - What word do you think these illustrations represent?

   - How did your classmates capture the meaning of the word in their illustrations?

   - Is there anything you would add or change to make the connection between the illustration and the word more meaningful to you?

8. Distribute copies of the *Our Illustrations* activity sheet (page 34) to students. Ask students to choose a picture from the other groups' chart paper and draw and describe it in the box on the left side of the paper.

9. Have each student create and describe his or her own independent illustration in the box on the right side of the activity sheet. Give students the option of combining two or more illustrations from their classmates in order to create new illustrations of their own.

10. Ask each student to create a new movement for each word. Then, have each student share his or her new movement with a partner.

Name: _____ Date: _____

Inherited Traits

Directions: Examine your family photograph. Mark the traits that you inherited from your mother and/or father with an *X*. If a trait is not shared with either parent, mark the *Neither* box.

	Mother	**Father**	**Neither**
Eye color			
Hair color			
Hair texture (e.g., curly, straight, wavy)			
Eye shape			
Face shape			

#51180—*Brain-Powered Lessons to Engage All Learners*

Hereditary Trait Cards

Teacher Directions: Cut apart the cards below. Place one card at each station.

parent

hereditary

inherited traits

acquired traits

Getting to the Point (of View)

Brain-Powered Strategy	**Standard**
It's All About Me	Understands the author's purpose or point of view

Vocabulary Words

- first person
- objective
- omniscient
- point of view
- third person

Materials

- *Point-of-View Sample Paragraphs* (pages 45–46)
- *Point-of-View Paragraph Notes* (page 47)
- *Point-of-View Sentences* (page 48)
- *Point-of-View Cards* (page 49)
- *Our Point-of-View Illustrations* (page 50)
- sample texts with different points of view
- chart paper and markers

Preparation Note: Make two copies of the *Our Point-of-View Illustrations* activity sheet (page 50) for each student. Additionally, cut apart the *Point-of-View Cards* (page 49).

Procedures

Model

1. Distribute the *Point-of-View Sample Paragraphs* and the *Point-of-View Paragraph Notes* activity sheets (pages 45–47) to students, and have them read the three paragraphs. Ask students to note the similarities and differences among the three paragraphs on the *Point-of-View Paragraph Notes* activity sheet.

2. Discuss the students' findings as a class, especially noting the different types of pronouns used in each paragraph. Using the *Point-of-View Sample Paragraphs* as a reference, explain the meaning of the term *point of view* and the differences between the terms *first person*, *third person*, *objective*, and *omniscient*.

3. Distribute the *Point-of-View Sentences* activity sheet (page 48) to each student. Explain to students that you will be presenting an action. Working in pairs, students should then practice writing sentences that describe the action you depicted from the different perspectives of the activity sheet.

4. Explain the *It's All About Me* strategy to students. (For detailed information on this strategy, see page 12.) Explain to students that they will create different movements relating to the following terms: *point of view*, *first person*, *third person*, *objective*, and *omniscient*. Think aloud while you develop a movement to represent the term *point of view* as an example for students.

Getting to the Point (of View) *(cont.)*

5. On the board, draw a picture that relates to the meaning of *point of view*. Remind students that illustrations are another tool that can help them remember the meanings of new words.

Apply/Analyze

6. Arrange the desks into four stations and divide students evenly among them. At each station, place one card from the *Point-of-View Cards* as well as several texts containing examples of this type of point of view. Have students use the *It's All About Me* strategy to create their own movements and illustrations that will allow them to personally connect the new term to its meaning.

7. Distribute a sheet of chart paper to each group. Ask students at each station to record their illustrations on a sheet of chart paper. Instruct students to write the word on the back of the paper in pencil. Students at each group should also dispose of their assigned *Point-of-View Cards*.

Evaluate/Create

8. Help students rotate from station to station so they can review the other groups' chart papers. Ask students to consider the following questions as they examine their classmates' illustrations at each station:

- What word or term do you think these illustrations represent?

- How did your classmates capture the meaning of the word in their illustrations?

- Is there anything you would add or change to make the connection between the illustration and the term more meaningful to you?

9. Give each student a copy of the *Our Point-of-View Illustrations* activity sheet (page 50). Ask each student to choose a picture from the other groups' chart paper and draw and describe it in the box on the left side of his or her activity sheet.

10. On the right side of the activity sheet, have students create and describe their own illustrations of the words. If they want, students may combine two or more illustrations from their classmates to create a new drawing.

11. Ask each student to create a new movement for each term. Then, have each student share his or her new movement with a partner.

Name: _____   Date: _____

Point-of-View Sample Paragraphs

Directions: Read paragraphs 1, 2, and 3. Take notes on the similarities and differences between the paragraphs on the next page.

Paragraph 1

The sunlight streaming through my window slowly dragged me from my slumber. I knew I needed to get up, but I really did not want to. I cracked open my eyes and glanced around. My clothes lay piled in a heap on the floor, and papers and books covered my desk. A brown banana peel balanced on the edge of the trash can, and an empty water bottle lay on its side. Familiar feelings of anxiety began to creep into my head. I closed my eyes and pretended to be asleep again.

Paragraph 2

The sunlight streaming through the bedroom window landed on Samantha's face, and she grumbled in her sleep. She slowly opened her eyes and looked around. Clothes lay piled in a heap on the floor, and papers and books covered the desk. A brown banana peel balanced on the edge of the trash can, and an empty water bottle lay on its side. She quickly closed her eyes again.

Name: _____   Date: _____

Point-of-View Sample Paragraphs (cont.)

Paragraph 3

The sunlight streaming through the bedroom window landed on Samantha's face, and she grumbled in her sleep. She knew she needed to get up, but she really did not want to. She slowly opened her eyes and looked around. Clothes lay piled in a heap on the floor, and papers and books covered the desk. A brown banana peel balanced on the edge of the trash can, and an empty water bottle lay on its side. She felt the familiar feelings of anxiety begin to creep into her head. She quickly closed her eyes and pretended to be asleep again.

Name: _____ Date: _____

Point-of-View Paragraph Notes

Similarities

_____

_____

_____

_____

_____

_____

Differences

_____

_____

_____

_____

_____

_____

_____

It's All About Me

Name: _____ Date: _____

Point-of-View Sentences

Directions: Observe the action performed by your teacher. Write two sentences describing the action, using the three different points of view listed below.

First person:_____

_____

Third person objective:_____

_____

Third person omniscient: _____

Action #1

_____

First person:_____

_____

Third person objective:_____

_____

Third person omniscient: _____

Action #2

_____

Point-of-View Cards

Teacher Directions: Cut apart the cards below. Place one at each station.

first person

third person

objective

omniscient

Name: _____ Date: _____

Our Point-of-View Illustrations

. . . .

Directions: Write the provided word at each station, and draw a picture of one illustration created by one of your classmates. Below each picture, describe the drawing, using words. Then, draw and describe your own illustration in the box in the column on the right.

Group Illustrations	My Illustrations
Word:	
_____	_____
_____	_____
Word:	
_____	_____
_____	_____

Data Displays

Brain-Powered Strategy

It Takes Two

Standards

Reads and interprets simple bar graphs, pie charts, and line graphs

Understands that data come in many different forms and that collecting, organizing, and displaying data can be done in many ways

Vocabulary Words

- bar graph
- data
- line graph
- pie chart

Materials

- *Mountain Elementary School Data* (page 53)
- *Comparing School Data* (page 54)
- *Our Feedback* (page 55)
- *Desert Elementary School Data* (page 56)
- *Triple Venn Diagram* (page 57)
- chart paper and markers
- pads of sticky notes in two different colors

Preparation Note: Prior to the lesson, create a two-column class T-chart on a sheet of chart paper or on the board. Label the left-hand column of the T-chart *Similarities* and the right-hand column *Differences*.

Procedures

Model

1. Poll the girls and boys separately about their favorite season of the year. Use the collected data to complete a bar graph, using different-color bars to show the data for the boys and the girls.

2. Ask students to examine the bar graph for similarities and differences in the data. Using the *It Takes Two* strategy, write each observed similarity and difference on a sticky note and place it in the correct column on the previously prepared T-chart. (For detailed information on this strategy, see page 13.)

3. Discuss the placement of the sticky notes, and model how to use sticky notes of different colors to write constructive comments and ideas on the chart.

Data Displays *(cont.)*

Apply/Analyze

4. Divide students into four groups. Provide each group with a copy of the *Mountain Elementary School Data* activity sheet (page 53).

5. Distribute copies of the *Comparing School Data* activity sheet (page 54) and stacks of two different-color sticky notes to each group. Instruct students to use the *It Takes Two* strategy to compare the classroom and Mountain Elementary School graphs' similarities and differences on the *Comparing School Data* activity sheet.

Evaluate/Create

6. Instruct students to leave their *Comparing School Data* activity sheets at their desks, and rotate to the next group so they can review the similarities and differences noted by the other groups in the class.

7. Distribute copies of the *Our Feedback* activity sheet (page 55) to each group, and have students read each group's activity sheet and complete an *Our Feedback* activity sheet to leave for the group. Ask students to consider the following questions:

- Do you agree or disagree with your classmates' choices?

- Are there any changes you would make?

If there are disagreements or recommendations of changes, they should note the difference on a different-color sticky note to add to a deeper discussion.

8. Allow the groups to review the feedback provided on the *Our Feedback* activity sheets and make revisions, as necessary.

9. Provide each student with a *Desert Elementary School Data* activity sheet (page 56) and a *Triple Venn Diagram* activity sheet (page 57). Discuss how to read the data on the pie charts. Have students work independently to compare your school's data, the pie charts from Desert Elementary, and Mountain Elementary School's graph, using the *Triple Venn Diagram* activity sheet.

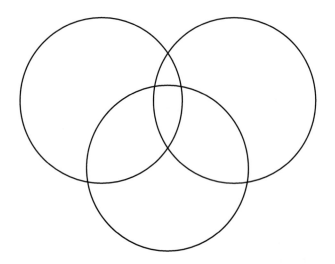

Name: _____ Date: _____

Mountain Elementary School Data

Directions: Examine the line graph below. How does the data on this graph compare to the data collected in your classroom? Write each similarity and difference on a separate sticky note and place it in the appropriate column on the class T-chart your teacher prepared.

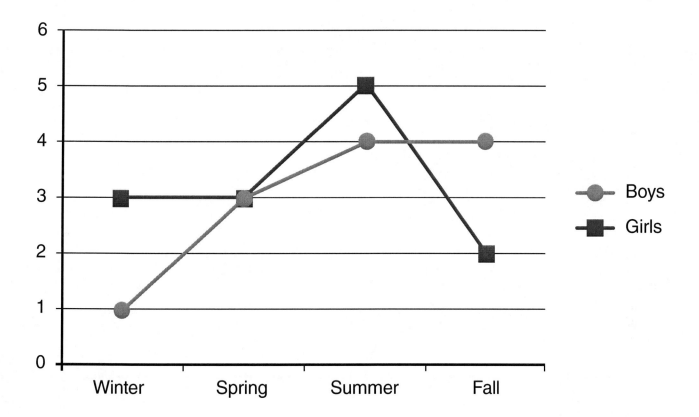

Name: _____ Date: _____

Comparing School Data

Directions: Write the names of the two sets of data you will be comparing on the lines at the top of the chart. On sticky notes, write the similarities and differences that you notice. Place each sticky note in the appropriate column.

_____ and _____	
Similarities	**Differences**

 #51180—Brain-Powered Lessons to Engage All Learners

Group Name: _____   Date: _____

Our Feedback

· ·

Directions: Discuss another group's chart. Record your responses here.

What We Agree With, and Why	What We Disagree With, and Why

Name: _____   Date: _____

Desert Elementary School Data

Directions: Examine the data in the two pie charts below.

Boys

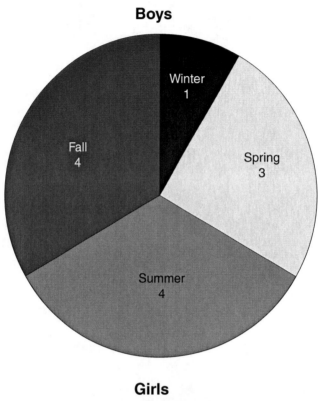

Girls

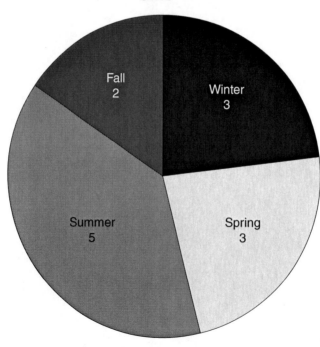

Name: _____   Date: _____

Triple Venn Diagram

Directions: Compare and contrast the three sets of school data. Make notes about shared features in the overlapping areas among the circles.

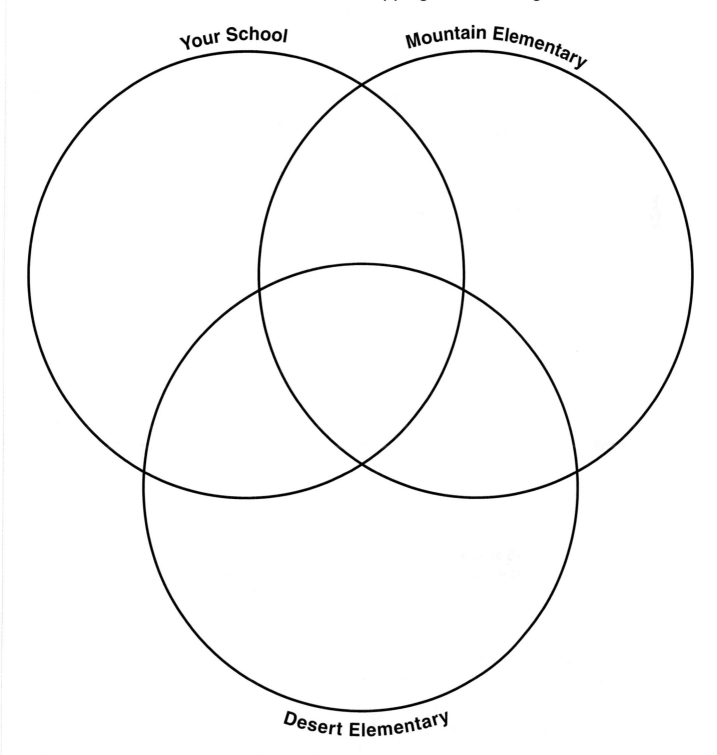

Stars and Planets: Same or Different?

Brain-Powered Strategy	**Standard**
It Takes Two	Understands the composition and structure of the universe and the Earth's place in it

Vocabulary Words

- moon
- planet
- star

Materials

- *Comparing Celestial Bodies* (page 60)
- *Our Feedback* (page 55)
- *Triple Venn Diagram* (page 61)
- chart paper and markers
- highlighers (*optional*)
- large pictures of two different planets (e.g., Saturn, Earth, Mars, Jupiter)
- stacks of sticky notes (two different colors)
- copies of short informational texts about planets and stars
- informational text about moons

Preparation Note: Prior to the lesson, create a two-column class T-chart on a sheet of chart paper or on the board. Label the left-hand column of the T-chart *Similarities* and the right-hand column *Differences*.

Procedures

Model

1. Display pictures of two different planets, and ask students to make observations about the physical similarities and differences between the two planets. Record each idea on a sticky note.

2. Use the *It Takes Two* strategy to observe any similarities and differences on sticky notes, and place them in the correct column on the prepared T-chart. (For detailed information on this strategy, see page 13.)

3. Model how to use sticky notes of a different color to write constructive comments about the ideas on the chart, including agreements or disagreements about the placement of sticky notes.

Stars and Planets: Same or Different? *(cont.)*

Apply/Analyze

4. Divide students into four groups, and provide each group with a variety of short informational texts on stars and planets. Have each student read a text and highlight, underline, or take notes about the important features of either stars or planets.

5. Distribute one copy of the *Comparing Celestial Bodies* activity sheet (page 60) and stacks of sticky notes (one color) to each group. Have the group members sit in a circle and take turns sharing the facts they learned about stars and planets. Working together, have the group members use the *It Takes Two* strategy to record the facts on sticky notes and place them on the activity sheet.

Evaluate/Create

6. Instruct students to leave their *Comparing Celestial Bodies* activity sheets at their desks and rotate clockwise to the next group.

7. Distribute copies of the *Our Feedback* activity sheet (page 55) to each group. Have students read the next group's activity sheet and complete an *Our Feedback* activity sheet to leave for the group. Ask students to consider the following questions:

- Do you agree or disagree with your classmates' choices?

- Are there any changes you would make?

If there are disagreements or recommendations of changes, encourage students to record their thoughts on different-color sticky notes and attach them in the appropriate locations.

8. Allow the groups to review the feedback provided on the *Our Feedback* activity sheets and make revisions, as necessary. Have the groups discuss how their thinking has changed based on the feedback from others in the class.

9. Display a blank T-chart at the front of the class. Have students work together to compile the ideas from their group comparison charts to create a classroom chart detailing the similarities and differences between planets and stars.

10. Provide each student with a *Triple Venn Diagram* activity sheet (page 61), and an informational text about moons to read independently. As a whole class, discuss the similarities and differences between planets, stars, and moons and add the new information to the classroom comparison chart as well as to the *Triple Venn Diagram* activity sheet.

Name: _____ Date: _____

Comparing Celestial Bodies

Directions: Write the names of the two things that you will be comparing on the lines at the top of the chart. On sticky notes, write the similarities and differences that you notice. Place each sticky note in the appropriate column.

_____ and _____	
Similarities	**Differences**

Name: _____ Date: _____

Triple Venn Diagram

Directions: Compare and contrast the stars, the planets, and the moon. Make notes about shared features in the overlapping areas among the circles.

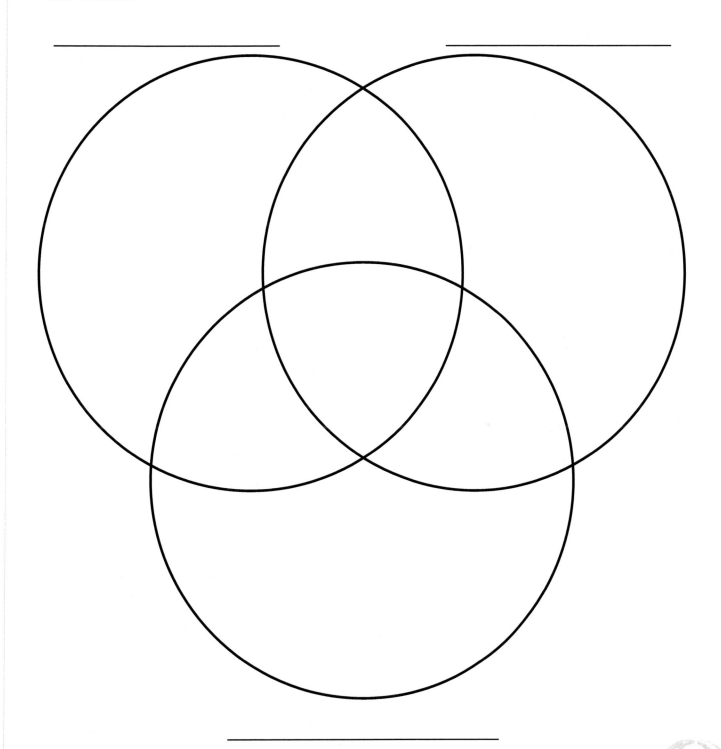

Mastering the Main Idea

Brain-Powered Strategy	Standard
It Takes Two	Determine the main idea of a text; recount the key details, and explain how they support the main idea

Vocabulary Words

- key details
- main idea
- summarize

Materials

- *Mixed-Up Paragraph #1* (page 64)
- *Mixed-Up Paragraph #2* (page 65)
- *Main Idea and Key Details Chart* (page 66)
- *Comparing Main Ideas and Key Details* (page 67)
- *Our Feedback* (page 55)
- sentence strips
- chart paper and markers
- sticky notes in two different colors
- copies of two brief informational articles on the same topic

Preparation Note: Prior to the lesson, prepare sentence strips ahead of time by writing one sentence from the *Mixed-Up Paragraph #1* (page 64) on each sentence strip. Additionally, create a two-column T-chart on a sheet of chart paper or on the board. Label the left-hand column of the T-chart *Similarities* and the right-hand column *Differences*.

Procedures

Model

1. Read the *Mixed-Up Paragraph #1* aloud to the class, and ask them why it does not make sense. Discuss how the organization of a paragraph helps the reader understand the concepts presented in the text.

2. Display the previously prepared sentence strips containing the sentences from the jumbled paragraph. Have students work together to rearrange the sentences until the paragraph makes sense. Explain to students that they will determine which sentence represents the main idea and which sentences contain key details.

Mastering the Main Idea *(cont.)*

3. Distribute the *Mixed-Up Paragraph #2* activity sheet (page 65), and ask students to repeat the activity independently.

4. Display the previously prepared T-chart to students. Read the main idea sentences from the two paragraphs aloud and ask students if these main ideas are similar or different. Using the *It Takes Two* strategy, record the similarities and differences on sticky notes and attach them to the T-chart. (For detailed information on this strategy, see page 13.) Repeat this process with the key details.

5. Model how to use sticky notes of a different color to write constructive comments about the ideas on the chart.

Apply/Analyze

6. Divide students into four groups and give half of the students in each group one informational article and the other half another article on the same topic. Have students read their articles independently.

7. Distribute two copies of the *Main Idea and Key Details Chart* activity sheet (page 66) to each group. Divide each group into two smaller groups according to which article students read, and ask students to work together to summarize the article on the chart.

8. Once both halves of the group have completed their charts, give each group one copy of the *Comparing Main Ideas and Key Details* activity sheet (page 67) and a stack of sticky notes (one color). Have students use the *It Takes Two* strategy to record the similarities and differences between the two articles.

Evaluate/Create

9. Ask students to leave their *Comparing Main Ideas and Key Details* activity sheets on their desks. Distribute one copy of the *Our Feedback* activity sheet (page 55) to each group, and have students rotate around the classroom, discussing each group's chart and completing the activity sheet to leave for the group. Ask students to consider the following questions:

- Do you agree or disagree with your classmates' choices?

- Are there any changes you would make?

In addition to completing the *Our Feedback* activity sheet, students may also record their suggestions and/or disagreements on different-color sticky notes that can be directly affixed to the group's comparison chart.

10. Allow the groups to review the feedback provided on the *Our Feedback* activity sheets and make revisions, as necessary.

11. After reviewing and incorporating the feedback, ask each student to summarize the similarities and differences between the two articles in two short paragraphs on a separate sheet of paper.

Mixed-Up Paragraph #1

Teacher Directions: Read the following paragraph aloud to the class. Discuss why it does not make sense.

They scavenge for their food at night and are primarily nocturnal animals. They have black rings around their tails and black "masks" around their eyes. They make their dens in holes, fallen trees, and household attics. Raccoons live in cities, prairies, marshes, and forests all over North America. The North American raccoon is a highly-adaptable mammal. Raccoons like to eat a wide variety of food, including plants, insects, fish, eggs, and garbage.

Name: _____   Date: _____

Mixed-Up Paragraph #2

Directions: Read the paragraph below. Underline the main idea and write the numbers 1, 2, and 3 next to three different key details. In the space below, rewrite the sentences from the paragraph so that the paragraph makes sense.

Their distinctive black and white stripes make them easy to identify. Predators know to stay away if they want to avoid getting sprayed. These mammals are nocturnal and often live in abandoned holes, hollow logs, and buildings. Their diets include small mammals, plants, insects, eggs, and even fish. Skunks inhabit most parts of North America and live in rural and urban areas. Skunks are notorious for the strong odor they spray when they feel threatened. Skunks have adapted their living habits and diets to accommodate a wide range of environments and conditions.

_____

_____

_____

_____

_____

_____

_____

_____

Name: _____ Date: _____

Main Idea and Key Details Chart

Directions: Read your article thoroughly. Write the main idea and key details from the article in the correct boxes below.

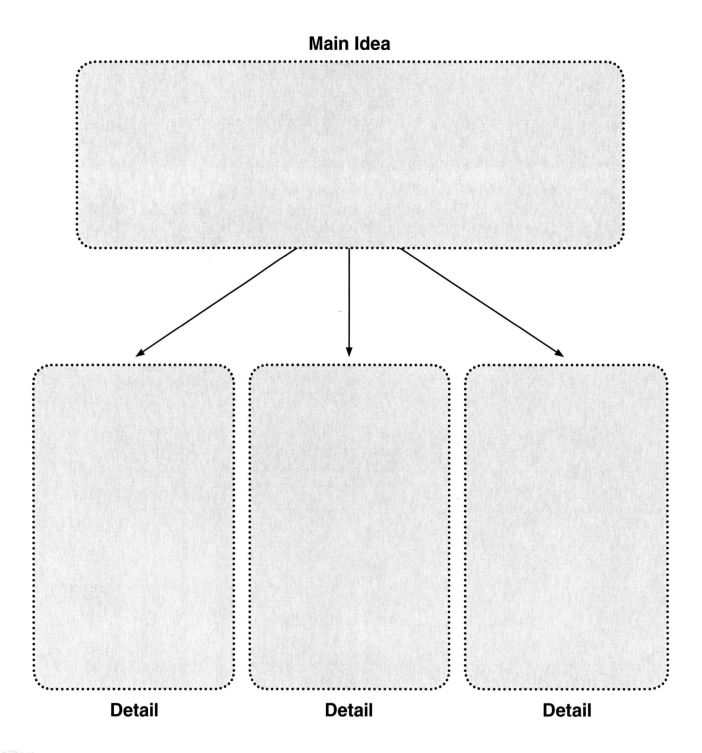

Main Idea

Detail   **Detail**   **Detail**

Name: _____ Date: _____

Comparing Main Ideas and Key Details

Directions: Write the names of the two articles you will be comparing on the lines at the top of the chart. On sticky notes, write the similarities and differences that you notice. Place each sticky note in the appropriate column.

_____ and _____

Similarities	Differences

The Power of the Law

Brain-Powered Strategy	Standard
That's a Wrap!	Knows the major responsibilities of the legislative, executive, and judicial branches of his or her state government

Vocabulary Words

- executive branch
- governor
- judicial branch
- legislative branch

Materials

- *The Three Branches of Government* (page 70)
- small slips of paper labeled with one of the three branches of government
- bowl
- three pieces of paper labeled with one of the branches of government (*executive*, *judicial*, *legislative*)
- index cards
- hole punch
- yarn or metal rings
- materials to make props and costumes (*optional*)

Preparation Note: Before beginning the lesson, cut enough small strips of paper so that each student will have one. Divide the slips of paper into three roughly equal groups and label each group with one of three branches of government. Fold the slips of paper in half and place them in a bowl.

Procedures

Model

1. Have each student pick a slip of paper from a bowl that assigns him or her a branch of government. Ask students to stand in groups under the paper labeled with their assigned branches (*executive*, *judicial*, *legislative*).

2. Briefly review the responsibilities of each branch of the state government. Then, tell students in the legislative branch that it is their responsibility to come up with a new classroom rule (law). Help the legislative group develop a rule and share it with the rest of the class.

The Power of the Law (cont.)

3. Have the judicial and executive branches share how they would change, enforce, or contribute to the creation and enactment of this new rule. Discuss the system of checks and balances.

4. Tell students that there are many different ways to study and today they will be learning a new way. Explain the *That's a Wrap!* strategy. (For detailed information on this strategy, see page 14.)

5. Model how to choose important facts and turn them into questions and answers, using complete sentences.

Apply/Analyze

6. Arrange the students into groups of three. Distribute copies of *The Three Branches of Government* activity sheet (page 70) to students. Assign each student in the group a government branch, and have the students write facts about their assigned branch in the appropriate box of their *The Three Branches of Government* activity sheet.

7. Instruct students to share their facts with the other two members in their groups and complete the rest of the boxes.

8. Distribute several index cards to each student. Using the facts from *The Three Branches of Government* activity sheet, ask students to write several questions and answers on their index cards, making sure to use complete sentences. Use a hole punch and join the cards with yarn or a metal ring. Tell students that they will use these questions later to write a script for a mock interview.

Evaluate/Create

9. Have students work in small groups to determine their roles for the interview. They can choose famous people or pretend characters that relate to the three branches of state government. Students can practice asking each other questions to prepare for the interview.

10. Allow students to make props and costumes to enhance the interview experience.

11. Give each group an opportunity to be interviewed by those in the audience. The audience should ask questions they heard from the presenters' script. Encourage presenters not to look at their scripts for the answers so that they begin to understand the difference between *know* and *still need to learn*. At the end of each interview, have the students shout, "That's a Wrap!"

12. Encourage students to use the index cards for further study at home. Students can quiz themselves or ask a friend or family member to ask questions from the cards to help them study.

Name: _____   Date: _____

The Three Branches of Government

Directions: Record several facts about your assigned government branch in the box below. Discuss the branches with your group, and fill in facts for the other two branches.

State Constitution		
Legislative	**Judicial**	**Executive**

Water: A Case of Multiple Identities

Brain-Powered Strategy	**Standard**
That's a Wrap!	Knows that water exists in the air in different forms and changes from one form to another through various processes

Vocabulary Words

- condensation
- evaporation
- freezing
- phase changes
- precipitation

Materials

- *Water Word Web* (page 73)
- blank strips of paper to create sentence strips
- index cards
- informational resources on the topic
- hole punch
- yarn or metal rings
- materials for making props/costumes (*optional*)

Procedures

Model

1. Distribute a *Water Word Web* activity sheet (page 73) to each student, and ask them to record information that they already know about the various phase changes of water.

2. Duplicate the word web on the board, and record students' ideas to create a class word web. Encourage students to add to their individual webs as their classmates share their ideas.

3. Tell students that there are many different ways to study and today they will be learning a new way. Explain the *That's a Wrap!* strategy to students. (For detailed information on this strategy, see page 14.)

4. Have students help you translate the information from the word web into factual statements and record these statements onto sentence strips.

5. Help students rearrange the sentence strips to show the importance of each fact. Discuss what makes some facts more important than others.

6. Choose a few of the recorded facts, and model how to turn them into questions and answers using complete sentences.

Water: A Case of Multiple Identities *(cont.)*

Apply/Analyze

7. Distribute several index cards to each student. Provide students with informational resources, books, articles, posters, study guides, notes, etc. about the processes that change water from one form to another. Have students study the information and then write questions on the front of their index cards and the corresponding answers on the back of the cards.

8. Use a hole punch and join the cards with yarn or a metal ring. Tell students that they will use these questions later to write a script for a mock interview.

Evaluate/Create

9. Have students work in small groups to determine their roles for the interview. They can choose famous people, someone they know at school, or pretend characters that relate to the matter. For example, they might choose to be a local television meteorologist, Mr. Hail, or Ms. Evaporation.

10. Give students the opportunity to create props and costumes to enhance the interview experience.

11. Allow groups an opportunity to be interviewed by the audience using the questions from the script they developed. Encourage presenters not to look at their scripts for the answers so that they begin to understand the difference between *know* and *still need to learn*. At the end of each interview, have students shout, "That's a Wrap!"

12. Allow students to take the index cards home and use them as a study tool. Students can quiz themselves or ask a friend or family member to ask them questions.

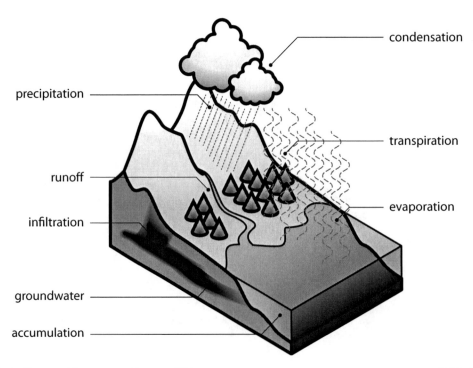

precipitation

runoff

infiltration

groundwater

accumulation

condensation

transpiration

evaporation

Name: _____ Date: _____

Water Word Web

Directions: Brainstorm words and ideas about the topics in the word web below.

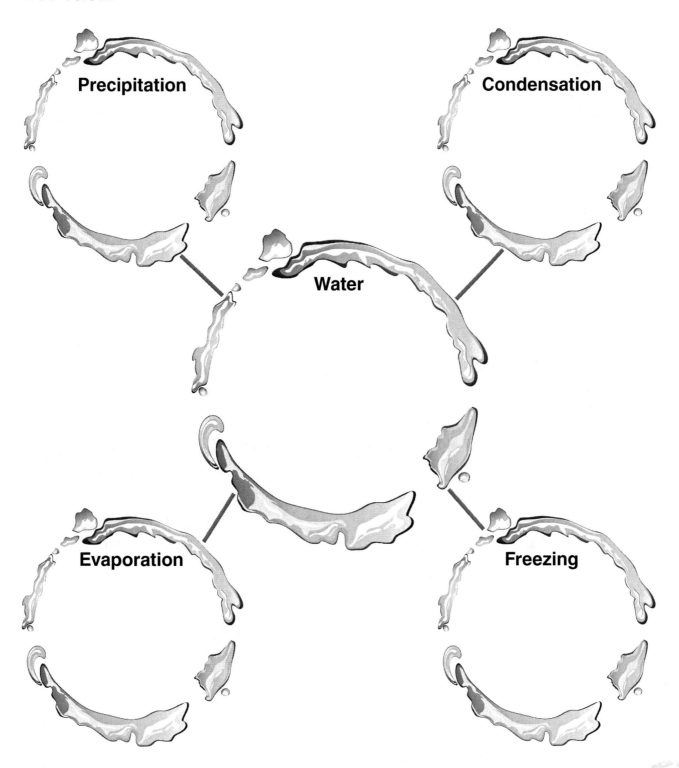

Find Me a Reference

Brain-Powered Strategy	Standard
That's a Wrap!	Ask and answer questions to demonstrate understanding of a text, referring explicitly to the text as the basis for the answers

Vocabulary Words

- citation
- explicit text reference
- text support

Materials

- *Notes and Text References* (page 76)
- picture book (e.g., *Thank You, Mr. Falker* by Patricia Polacco)
- variety of books, articles, notes, and other reference materials on a topic of your choice
- index cards
- hole punch
- yarn or metal rings
- materials to make props or costumes (*optional*)

Procedures

Model

1. Read the picture book aloud to the class. Ask students how the main character feels at the beginning, middle, and end of the story.

2. Model how to go through the book and explicitly reference the text and illustrations to determine the main character's feelings. Record the text citations, including page numbers on the board, and discuss how these references provide support for the students' answers.

3. Tell students that there are many different ways to study and today they will be learning a new way. Explain the *That's a Wrap!* strategy to students. (For detailed information on this strategy, see page 14.)

4. Explain the difference between more-important ideas and less-important ideas. Help students rank the importance of each idea from the story.

5. Choose a few of the recorded facts, and model how to turn them into questions and answers, using complete sentences.

Find Me a Reference *(cont.)*

Apply/Analyze

6. Provide students with a variety of books, articles, notes, and other reference materials on a topic of your choice. Distribute a *Notes and Text References* activity sheet (page 76) to each student, and ask them to use the research materials to take notes on the topic.

7. Distribute the index cards to students. Using their notes, have students write questions on the front sides of the index cards and the corresponding answers on the backs. Encourage students to explicitly reference the text in their answers.

8. Use a hole punch and join the cards with yarn or a metal ring. Tell students that they will use these questions later to write scripts for mock interviews.

Evaluate/Create

9. Have students work in small groups to determine their roles for the interview. They can choose famous people, someone they know at school, or pretend characters that relate to the matter. For example, they can pretend to be famous authors.

10. Provide students with the opportunity to create props and/or costumes for the interviews.

11. Allow groups opportunities to be interviewed by the students in the audience, using questions from the scripts they developed. Encourage presenters not to look at their scripts for the answers so that they begin to understand the difference between *know* and *still need to learn*. At the end of each interview, have students shout, "That's a Wrap!"

12. Have students take the index cards home to use for studying.

Name: _____ Date: _____

Notes and Text References

Directions: As you read through the reference materials, take notes on the left side of the chart. Record the page number where you found the information in the right column. Then, write the most important ideas or facts from the text in the space at the bottom of the page.

Notes	Text Reference

Most important ideas or facts:

Map Experts

Brain-Powered Strategy	Standard
ABC Professors	Knows major physical and human features of places as they are represented on maps and globes

Vocabulary Words

- human feature
- icons
- physical feature
- symbols

Materials

- *Map Feature Cards* (pages 79–82)
- *Map Feature Examples Chart* (pages 83–84)
- *ABC Professor Notes* (page 85)
- examples of maps and globes with physical and human features
- lab coats or geography badges (*optional*)
- chart paper (*optional*)

Preparation Note: Prior to the lesson, cut apart the *Map Feature Cards* (pages 79–82).

Procedures

Model

1. Distribute one card from the *Map Feature Cards* to each student. Tell students they will each need to find the partner with the card that matches his or her own card. For example, if the card has a word, they will need to find the card with the corresponding icon and vice versa.

2. Discuss the difference between a physical feature and a human feature. Designate one side of the room for physical features and the other side for human features. Ask students to stand up and move to the appropriate side of the room according to the cards that they are holding.

3. Provide each side of the room with several examples of maps or globes showing either physical or human features. Distribute copies of the *Map Feature Examples Chart* activity sheet (pages 83–84) to students. Ask each pair of students to find an example of the feature on its card on the map and record it on the activity sheet.

4. Have students walk around the room and exchange examples with their classmates to complete their charts.

Map Experts *(cont.)*

5. Explain that each student is now a "geography genius" because they are experts at reading and understanding the human and physical features on maps and globes. (Provide students with lab coats or special geography badges, if desired.) Describe the *ABC Professors* strategy to the class. (For detailed information on this strategy, see page 15.)

6. Model the strategy for students using a replica of the *ABC Professor Notes* activity sheet (page 85) on the board or on a sheet of chart paper.

Apply/Analyze

7. Divide students into pairs and give each pair a copy of the *ABC Professor Notes* activity sheet. You may wish to use an enlarged version of the chart on this activity sheet found on the Digital Resource CD (filename: abcnotes.pdf). Have each pair of students work together to complete the sheet, using the strategy.

Evaluate/Create

8. Combine the pairs of students to make groups of four. Have students share their responses with everyone in the group and provide positive feedback. Encourage students to add to their notes when they hear new words or phrases. Ask students to consider the following questions when discussing their notes:

- How do these words and phrases relate to geography?

- What are other words or phrases you could include in the boxes?

- Were you able to think of more physical features or human features?

9. Have students return to their original partners and distribute a second copy of the *ABC Professor Notes* activity sheet to each student. Have students repeat the activity again but this time writing topic-related questions that begin with the letter instead of words or phrases. If there are space constraints, you may wish to have students use a separate sheet of paper to write their questions. Provide students with examples of questions, and then have them complete the sheets.

10. Introduce the concept of higher-order questions using Bloom's Revised Taxonomy or Kaplan's work. (For information on higher-order questions, see pages 22–23.) Model how to use question stems and encourage students to create questions at various levels.

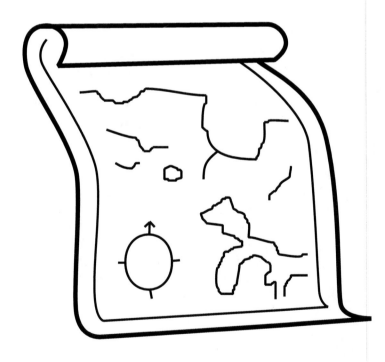

Map Feature Cards

Teacher Directions: Cut apart the cards below. Give one to each student.

# river	
# lake	
# desert	
# mountain	

Map Feature Cards *(cont.)*

beach	
waterfalls	
wetlands	
ocean currents	

Map Feature Cards (cont.)

restaurant	
park	
restroom	
information center	

Map Feature Cards (cont.)

fire station	
hospital	
historical landmarks	
bank	

Name: _____   Date: _____

Map Feature Examples Chart

Directions: Fill in the example for your card. Then, share with other students to complete the example column.

Example								
Icon								
Name	river	lake	desert	mountain	beach	waterfall	wetlands	ocean current

Name: _____   Date: _____

Map Feature Examples Chart (cont.)

Example								
Icon	🍽	🎠	🚻	ℹ	🚒	H	⚔	$
Name	restaurant	park	restroom	information center	fire station	hospital	historic landmark	bank

Name: _____ Date: _____

ABC Professor Notes

Directions: Think of something that relates to the topic your teacher gave you. What letter does that word start with? Find that box, and write or draw it in the box.

A	B	C	D	E
F	G	H	I	J
K	L	M	N	O
P	Q	R	S	T
U	V	W	X	Y
Z				

Mass Wizards

Brain-Powered Strategy	**Standard**
ABC Professors	Measure and estimate masses of objects using standard units of grams (*g*)

Vocabulary Words

- estimate
- grams
- kilograms
- mass

Materials

- *My Estimates Chart* (page 88)
- *ABC Professor Notes* (page 89)
- gram units or paper clips
- pineapple
- various objects to measure (one for every two students)
- balance
- "Mass Wizards" hats (*optional*)
- chart paper (*optional*)

Preparation Note: Make enough copies of the *My Estimates Chart* activity sheet (page 88) so that there are enough rows to make notes for each object used in the lesson.

Procedures

Model

1. Show students a paper clip and a pineapple. Explain that a paper clip has the mass of about one gram and the pineapple has the mass of about one kilogram.

2. Distribute a *My Estimates Chart* activity sheet to each student. Assign each student a partner, and give each pair an object from around the classroom. Have each student draw a picture of the object in the top row of the chart and estimate the mass of the object in grams or kilograms in the appropriate box. **Note:** Depending on the size of the balance, you may need to only measure the mass for smaller objects.

3. Instruct students to leave their objects on their desks. Have students walk around the classroom and complete their charts by drawing pictures and estimating the masses of the objects on student desks.

4. Once students have completed their estimation, ask pairs of students to come to the front of the class and use the balance to find the mass of their original objects. Have all students record the masses of the objects in the third column of the chart. **Note:** Use paper clips to measure the mass if you are unable to find gram units.

Mass Wizards *(cont.)*

5. Tell students that they are now known as "Mass Wizards" because they are experts at estimating and measuring the mass of objects. (Provide students with special hats to wear, if desired.) Explain the *ABC Professors* strategy to the class. (For detailed information on this strategy, see page 15.)

6. Model the strategy using a replica of the *ABC Professor Notes* activity sheet (page 89) on the board or chart paper.

Apply/Analyze

7. Divide students into pairs and distribute the *ABC Professor Notes* to each set of partners. You may wish to use an enlarged version of the chart on this activity sheet found on the Digital Resource CD (filename: abcnotes.pdf). Instruct students to think of examples of objects that have a mass of about one gram and one kilogram for each letter. Remind students that these are estimates.

Evaluate/Create

8. Combine pairs of students to make groups of four. Ask students to share the ideas they recorded on their activity sheets with the other group members. Encourage students to record new words on their activity sheets and provide their group members with positive feedback. Have students consider the following questions when they discuss as a group:

- What are other words or phrases you could include in the boxes?

- Was it easier to think of objects with a mass of one gram or one kilogram?

- Which boxes were the easiest/hardest to complete?

9. Tell students that they will complete a second *ABC Professor Notes* activity sheet, but this time they will fill in the boxes with topic-related questions that start with the letter in the box instead of words. If there are space constraints, you may wish to have students use a separate sheet of paper to write their questions. Provide students with examples of questions, and then have them complete the sheet.

10. Introduce students to the concept of Bloom's Revised Taxonomy or Kaplan's work and show them how to use question stems to create questions that address higher-order thinking skills. (For information on higher-order questions, see pages 22–23.)

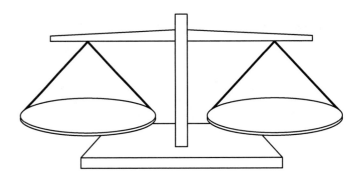

Name: _____ Date: _____

My Estimates Chart

. . . .

Directions: Draw a picture of each object in the first column. Write your estimate of the object's mass in the middle column. After it has been measured, record the object's mass in the third column.

Weight						
Estimated Mass						
Picture						

Name: _____ Date: _____

ABC Professor Notes

. . . .

Directions: Think of an object with a mass of approximately one gram and an object with a mass of approximately one kilogram. What letter does each object start with? Find that box, and write or draw it in the box.

A	B	C	D	E
F	G	H	I	J
K	L	M	N	O
P	Q	R	S	T
U	V	W	X	Y
Z				

Inquiry Tools

Brain-Powered Strategy	Standard
ABC Professors	Uses appropriate tools and simple equipment to gather scientific data and extend the senses

Vocabulary Words

- magnifier

- microscope

- scientific data

- thermometer

Materials

- *Scientific Tools Clues* (page 92)

- *ABC Professor Notes* (page 93)

- examples of scientific tools and equipment

- chart paper (*optional*)

Procedures

Model

1. Using the *Scientific Tools Clues* (page 92) as a guide, have students try to guess the scientific tools from the clues you read. Read one clue at a time. If no one guesses the answer, read the next clue. Once the tool has been guessed, write the word on the board and show them an actual example of the tool, if one is available.

2. Review the list of scientific tools on the board. Ask students to provide examples of how the tools are used, what they measure, and why the data is important for scientists.

3. Explain the *ABC Professors* strategy to the class. (For detailed information on this strategy, see page 15.)

4. Model the strategy, using a replica of the *ABC Professor Notes* activity sheet (page 93) on the board or on a sheet of chart paper. Demonstrate how to think of scientific tools and other words associated with the tools (e.g., thermometer, Celsius, Fahrenheit, freezing) and write those in the boxes according to their initial letter.

Inquiry Tools *(cont.)*

Apply/Analyze

5. Assign students partners and distribute a copy of the *ABC Professor Notes* activity sheet to each pair. You may wish to use an enlarged version of the chart on this activity sheet found on the Digital Resource CD (filename: abcnotes.pdf). Instruct students to take turns writing words related to scientific inquiry that start with the letter shown in each box. Remind students that these words can refer to scientific processes, equipment, units of measurement, etc.

Evaluate/Create

6. Assign students a new partner and have them share the words they recorded on their activity sheets with their partners. Encourage students to write, on their activity sheets, new words they hear, and provide their partners with positive feedback. Ask students to think about the following questions when discussing their activity sheets with their partners:

- What are other words or phrases you could include in the boxes?

- How do these words relate to the process of scientific inquiry?

- Which boxes were the easiest/hardest to complete?

- Which word do you think was your most creative contribution?

7. Tell students that they will complete a second *ABC Professor Notes* activity sheet, but this time they will fill in the boxes with topic-related questions that start with the letter in the box instead of words. If there are space constraints, you may wish to have students use a separate sheet of paper to write their questions. Provide students with examples of questions, and then have them complete the sheets.

8. Use Bloom's Revised Taxonomy question stems to encourage higher-order thinking and questions. (For information on higher-order questions, see pages 22–23.)

Scientific Tools Clues

Teacher Directions: Read each clue aloud and call on several students to provide guesses. If no one guesses the correct answer, read the next clue. Once the object is guessed, display an example of the object and write the word on the board.

Word: *thermometer*

1. I have two units of measurement.

2. My units of measurements are named for famous scientists.

3. Originally, I contained mercury.

4. You might need me if you get sick.

5. I measure temperature.

Word: *magnifier*

1. I can be made out of glass or plastic.

2. My invention led to the creation of eyeglasses.

3. I am convex.

4. I help people see things better.

5. I make images appear larger.

Word: *microscope*

1. I can be small enough to fit on your desk or big enough to take up an entire building.

2. I usually have an internal light source to illuminate the object of study.

3. I have a base, an arm, and a focus knob.

4. I have an eyepiece lens and one or more other lenses.

5. I am used to see things not visible to the naked eye.

Name: _____   Date: _____

ABC Professor Notes

··

Directions: Think of something that relates to the process of scientific inquiry. What letter does the word start with? Find that box, and write the word.

A	B	C	D	E
F	G	H	I	J
K	L	M	N	O
P	Q	R	S	T
U	V	W	X	Y
Z				

Event Sequencing

Brain-Powered Strategy	Standard
WPH Accordion	Establish a situation and introduce a narrator and/or characters

Vocabulary Words	Materials
• event sequence • narrative • predict	• *My Feedback* (page 96) • picture book • chart paper and markers (*optional*) • half-sheets of paper (cut horizontally) • student writing samples

Preparation Note: Prior to the lesson, have each student choose a personal-narrative writing sample to share with a partner. Ideally, this writing sample should be a completed but not yet revised draft.

Procedures

Model

1. Explain the *WPH Accordion* strategy to students. (For detailed information on this strategy, see page 16.) Tell students that they will be using this strategy in two different formats—to first examine the sequence of events in a storybook and then to improve their own narrative writing.

2. Introduce the book chosen for the lesson by showing students the cover and reading the title to them. Look through the first few pages, examining the illustrations and discussing possible topics for the book.

3. Draw a three-column chart on the board or on a sheet of chart paper. Label the columns *W*, *P*, and *H*, and draw symbols to remind students of the letters' significance (*W* = who or what, *P* = predict, and *H* = happens).

4. Read the selected story aloud to students and stop periodically to fill in the information on the chart. Make sure to highlight the order in which the events in the book unfolded and the role this sequence played in the overall effect of the story.

5. Explain to students that they will now have a chance to do this process themselves, but instead of using a storybook from the classroom library, they will use their classmates' written narratives. They will also use a slightly different format.

Event Sequencing *(cont.)*

Apply/Analyze

6. Distribute a half-sheet of paper to each student. Instruct students to fold the paper to create an accordion.

7. Have students turn the folded paper so that the first fold is on top. Leaving the first section blank for the title, show students how to label the following sections *W, P,* and *H,* and draw the corresponding symbols for each section.

8. Assign each student a partner, and have students switch narrative writing samples. Ask students to read the first paragraph of their partners' stories and then stop, write the titles of the stories on the fronts of the accordions, and complete the *W* and *P* sections. Then, have students finish reading the stories and complete the *H* section with the events that actually occurred in the stories.

Evaluate/Create

9. To debrief, ask students the following questions:

- Were your predictions on target?

- What clues did you miss that would have helped you with more accurate predictions?

- How did the sequence of events help you understand the story?

- How did prior knowledge help you learn new knowledge?

10. Distribute a copy of the *My Feedback* activity sheet (page 96) to each student, and ask students to answer the questions.

11. Have partners exchange feedback sheets and discuss them. Instruct students to revise their stories, incorporating their partners' feedback as they see fit. Another option is to have students write alternative endings to their stories based on the predictions their partners made on the accordions.

Name: _____   Date: _____

My Feedback

Directions: Provide your partner with positive feedback using the questions below.

1. Did the sequence of events unfold naturally? How could the story be improved to make the sequence of events seem more natural?

_____

_____

_____

_____

2. How did the sequence of events in the story help you predict what would happen next?

_____

_____

_____

_____

3. What were your favorite parts of the story? What other suggestions do you have for the author that could help improve the story?

_____

_____

_____

_____

Measurement Mania

Brain-Powered Strategy	Standard
WPH Accordion	Generate measurement data by measuring lengths using rulers marked with halves and fourths of an inch

Vocabulary Words

- fractional measurement
- half-inch
- quarter-inch

Materials

- objects to measure
- projector
- ruler
- chart paper (*optional*)
- half-sheets of paper (cut horizontally)
- colored pencils or crayons

Preparation Note: Prior to the lesson, gather items around the classroom for students to measure. Each student should receive one item.

Procedures

Model

1. Show students three objects and ask them to estimate the length of the objects to the nearest inch. Record students' estimations on the board, and then ask several students to measure the objects and record the actual lengths on the board.

2. Hold up two objects that are very similar in length but not quite the same (e.g., two pencils of slightly different lengths). Using a projector and a ruler, demonstrate how to measure the two objects using halves and quarters of an inch in order to make the measurements more accurate.

3. Explain the *WPH Accordion* strategy to students. (For detailed information on this strategy, see page 16.) Draw a three-column chart on the board or on a sheet of chart paper. Label the columns *W*, *P*, and *H*, and draw symbols to remind students of the letters' significance (*W* = who or what, *P* = predict, and *H* = happens).

4. Have students estimate the lengths of several other objects using fractional measurements. Record the names of the objects in the *W* column and the estimated lengths in the *P* column. Ask several students to come to the front of the class and, using the projector and a ruler, measure each object to the nearest quarter-inch. Record this data in the *H* column.

Measurement Mania *(cont.)*

5. Explain to students they will now have the chance to do this process themselves, using a slightly different format.

Apply/Analyze

6. Distribute a half-sheet of paper to each student and an object to measure. Instruct students to fold the paper to create an accordion.

7. Have each student write the name of his or her object on the first section of the accordion. Show students how to label the following sections *W*, *P*, and *H*, and draw the corresponding symbols for each section.

8. Have students complete their accordions with information about their objects.

Evaluate/Create

9. To debrief, ask students the following questions:

- Was your prediction on target?

- Is there anything you could have done to make your prediction more accurate?

- Was it easier to predict to the nearest inch or nearest quarter-inch? Why do you think this is?

- How did prior knowledge help you learn new knowledge?

10. Have each student create a new *WPH Accordion* activity sheet to complete at home. Ask students to select four objects and have friends, siblings, or relatives estimate the lengths of the objects to the nearest quarter-inch. Then, have the student record his or her own estimations next to these numbers. Lastly, have the student measure the objects to the nearest quarter-inch and record these measurements in the *H* column.

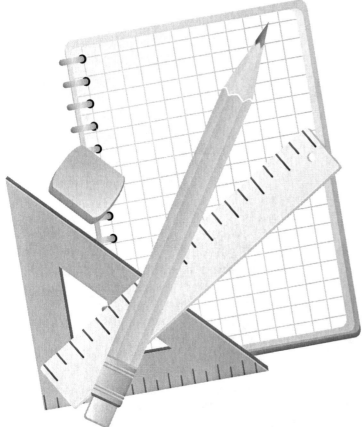

Take a Stance

Brain-Powered Strategy	Standard
WPH Accordion	Distinguish their own point of view from that of the author of a text

Vocabulary Words	**Materials**
• opinion • persuasive writing • point of view	• chart paper (*optional*) • example of persuasive writing on a controversial topic • half-sheets of paper (cut horizontally) • copies of two different articles representing both sides of a debate (one article per student)

Procedures

Model

1. Ask students an open-ended, debatable question such as, *What is the most important thing teachers should teach their students in school?* Hold a class discussion and allow students to express their opinions.

2. Explain the *WPH Accordion* strategy to students. (For detailed information on this strategy, see page 16.) Draw a three-column chart on the board or on a sheet of chart paper. Label the columns *W*, *P*, and *H*, and draw symbols to remind the students of the letters' significance (*W* = who or what, *P* = predict, and *H* = happens).

3. Select an article relating to the question from Step 1. Remind students that the purpose of persuasive writing is to express the author's opinion or point of view on a topic. Read the first paragraph or two aloud to the class.

4. Have students help complete the *W* and *P* columns of the chart. For the *P* column, ask students to predict what they think the author's point of view will be in the remainder of the article.

5. Read the rest of the article aloud. Have students summarize the author's point of view and main arguments in the *H* column on the chart.

6. Explain to students that they will now have the chance to use the *WPH Accordion* strategy independently, using a slightly different format.

Take a Stance *(cont.)*

Apply/Analyze

7. Distribute a half-sheet of paper to each student. Instruct students to fold the paper to create an accordion and label the sections *W*, *P*, and *H*.

8. Provide half of the students with an article expressing one side of a different controversial topic (e.g., should students be required to wear uniforms to school?) and the other half of the students with a similar article arguing the other side of the topic.

9. Have each student write the title of his or her article in the first section of the accordion. Ask students to read the first two paragraphs of their articles and then stop and complete the *W* and *P* sections of their accordions. Then, have them read the rest of the article and fill in the *H* section.

10. Assign each student a partner from the other group so that the opinions from both articles are represented. Have students share the author's point of view from the article they read and summarize the main arguments for their partners.

Evaluate/Create

11. To debrief, ask students the following questions:

- Were you able to correctly predict the author's point of view based on the two opening paragraphs?

- Did your prediction make sense?

- What clues helped make your prediction accurate? Did you miss any clues?

- How did prior knowledge help you learn new knowledge?

12. Have each student write about his or her own point of view on the controversial topic from Step 8. Ask each of them to describe how his or her point of view is similar to or different from the author's point of view.

Missing Links

Brain-Powered Strategy	**Standards**
Matchmaker	Use linking words and phrases to connect ideas within categories of information
	Use temporal words and phrases to signal event order

Vocabulary Words

- additional information
- conclusion
- contrast
- sequence of events
- temporal words

Materials

- *My Linking Words Chart* (page 103)
- *Linking Words Cards* (pages 104–107)
- *Missing Links* (page 108)
- address labels
- wordless comic strip
- projector

Preparation Note: Prior to the lesson, write the vocabulary words on address labels. Make enough labels so that each student will have one label to wear. Additionally, cut apart the *Linking Words Cards* (pages 104–107).

Procedures

Model

1. Display a wordless comic strip on the projector and ask students to describe what is happening in each frame. Write one sentence describing each frame on the board, and then read the sentences aloud. Ask students, "If I read these sentences aloud, does that sound like a well-written paragraph to you? What is missing that could make these sentences into a good paragraph?"

2. Discuss the importance of linking, or transition words, and the role they play in connecting ideas, thoughts, opinions, and details in good writing. Explain how these words can show the sequence of events or help summarize the author's thoughts. Linking words can also indicate a contrast between ideas, highlight additional information, or reveal information about the time something occurs.

3. Distribute the *My Linking Words Chart* activity sheet (page 103) to students and display a copy of the chart on a projector. As a class, brainstorm linking words for each category in the chart and record them on the chart.

Missing Links *(cont.)*

Apply/Analyze

4. Provide students with additional linking words and have them classify the words according to their function and write them in the appropriate box on the chart.

5. Divide students into groups of five. Give each student an address label with one vocabulary word on it to wear and explain the instructions for the activity. Guide students through the playing of the first round, using the *Linking Words Cards* (pages 104–107). You may wish to use larger versions of the cards found on the Digital Resource CD (filename: linkingwordscards.pdf). Explain the Matchmaker strategy to students (For detailed information on this strategy, see page 17.)

6. After completing the first round of the activity, have the groups switch sets of the *Linking Words Cards* and play again, as time allows.

Evaluate/Create

7. Distribute the *Missing Links* activity sheet (page 108) to students. Have students read the sentences, list the linking words they want to add to improve the paragraph, and then rewrite the paragraph, using the linking words.

8. Have students switch their *Missing Links* activity sheet with partners. Ask students to read each other's paragraph and discuss how the linking words were used to improve the paragraph.

9. Distribute writing paper to students. Have them write new paragraphs on topics of their choosing. Instruct them to use at least three linking words in their paragraph. Provide students with time to share their writing with classmates.

Name: _____ Date: _____

My Linking Words Chart

Directions: Write linking words in the appropriate boxes below.

Temporal Words

Sequence of Events

Additional Information

Contrasting Information

Concluding Words

Linking Words Cards

Teacher Directions: Cut apart the cards below. Give one set to each group of five students.

Set #1

soon	first... second... third...	additionally
however	in conclusion	

Linking Words Cards *(cont.)*

Set #2

then	at the beginning... then...at the end...	furthermore
on the other hand	hence	

Linking Words Cards (cont.)

Set #3

after	in the first place...also... finally...	moreover
on the contrary	therefore	

Linking Words Cards *(cont.)*

Set #4

later	to begin... then... lastly...	in addition
yet	to conclude	

Name: _____   Date: _____

Missing Links

Directions: Read the paragraph below. List the linking words you plan to add to the paragraph to improve it. Rewrite the paragraph, including the linking words in the space below.

The red-eyed tree frog lives in Central America and northern South America. These intensely colored frogs have large red eyes, orange feet, blue flanks, and bright-green bodies. They camouflage themselves during the day by closing their eyes and sleeping underneath leaves. Scientists think their coloration helps them in several ways. Their bright colors may help surprise predators and give the frogs a chance to escape. Predators may also assume that these frogs are poisonous because of their bright colors. They actually are not venomous. The red-eyed tree frog relies on its vivid coloration for its survival.

Linking words I plan to add to the paragraph: _____

_____

Improved Paragraph

_____

_____

_____

_____

_____

_____

_____

Where Am I?

Brain-Powered Strategy 🧑‍🤝‍🧑	**Standard**
Matchmaker	Knows the approximate location of major bodies of water on Earth

Vocabulary Words

- Arctic Ocean
- Atlantic Ocean
- Indian Ocean
- Pacific Ocean
- Southern Ocean

Materials

- *Ocean Facts* (pages 111–112)
- *My Ocean Notes* (page 113)
- *Ocean Names Cards* (page 114)
- *World Map* (page 115)
- address labels
- index cards with the names of the oceans
- world map (large) with ocean names hidden
- colored markers or pencils

Preparation Note: Prior to the lesson, write the vocabulary words on address labels. Make enough labels so that each student will have one label to wear. Additionally, cut apart the *Ocean Facts* (pages 111–112) and the *Ocean Names Cards* (page 114).

Procedures

Model

1. Randomly distribute one strip of paper from the *Ocean Facts* (pages 111–112) to each student. You may wish to use larger versions of the cards found on the Digital Resource CD (filename: oceanfacts.pdf). Have all of the students with the number one in front of their fact take turns reading their facts aloud. When all of the students with the number one have read their facts, have students guess which ocean these clues refer to and attach the labeled index card to the world map in the appropriate location. **Note:** If you have more than 24 students, you may wish to create more facts on index cards.

2. Continue to call the groups by number, and have students read their facts aloud. Once students identify the name of the ocean, add the label to the map until all five oceans are correctly labeled.

3. Review the names of the five oceans on the map and discuss their distinguishing characteristics. Distribute the *My Ocean Notes* activity sheet (page 113) to students, and have them record the important points about each ocean.

Where Am I? *(cont.)*

Apply/Analyze

4. Divide students into groups of five. Give each student an address label with one vocabulary word on it to wear. Have students stand in a circle and put a set of the *Ocean Names Cards* (page 114) on the floor in the middle of the circle. You may wish to use larger versions of the cards found on the Digital Resource CD (filename: oceannames.pdf).

5. Explain the instructions for the activity, and guide students through the playing of the round of the activity. Explain the *Matchmaker* strategy to students. (For detailed information on this strategy, see page 17.)

6. After completing the first round, have students mix up the cards and return them to the center of the circle. Tell students to switch address labels and then play again.

Evaluate/Create

7. Distribute copies of the *World Map* activity sheet (page 115) to students, and have them label the oceans, using different-color markers or colored pencils.

8. Assign each student a partner and have them work together to create a poem or song to help them remember the names of the five oceans. Encourage them to also include additional information about the various oceans.

9. Have students share their songs or poems aloud with the rest of the class. If possible, display them on a bulletin board so the students can continue to review them.

Answer Key

#1—Pacific Ocean

#2—Arctic Ocean

#3—Atlantic Ocean

#4—Indian Ocean

#5—Southern Ocean

Ocean Facts

Teacher Directions: Cut apart each strip. Distribute one fact to each student.

#1—I am the biggest ocean on Earth.	**#2**—Many polar bears live on the ice surrounding my waters.
#1—I cover more than 30 percent of Earth's surface.	**#2**—During the winter, I am almost completely covered in ice.
#1—I am the deepest ocean on Earth.	**#2**—I am the northernmost ocean.
#1—I touch the United States, Canada, China, Japan, Australia, Peru, Chile, and many other countries.	**#2**—I am the smallest ocean.
#1—I contain the Great Barrier Reef.	**#3**—I am the second-largest ocean on Earth.
#2—I am located around the North Pole.	**#3**—I touch the continents of North America, South America, Europe, and Africa.

Ocean Facts *(cont.)*

#3—I contain the Caribbean islands.

#4—I am named for one of the countries I border.

#3—The longest mountain range in the world runs through me from Iceland to Antarctica.

#5—I am located around the South Pole.

#4—I touch the continents of Africa, Antarctica, Asia, and Australia.

#5—I am home to the emperor penguin.

#4—I am the world's largest breeding ground for humpback whales.

#5—I encircle Antarctica.

#4—I contain an important trade route for oil that travels from the Middle East to Asia.

#5—I was only designated an ocean in the year 2000.

#4—I am the third-largest ocean.

#5—I am the fourth-largest ocean.

Name: _____   Date: _____

My Ocean Notes

Directions: Use the chart below to record notes about Earth's five oceans.

Ocean Name	Notes

Ocean Names Cards

Teacher Directions: Copy and cut apart five sets of these cards. Give one set to each group of five students.

I am the largest ocean on Earth.	I surround Antarctica.
I touch the continents of Asia, Australia, and Africa.	I am the second-largest ocean.
I am the northernmost ocean.	

Name: _____ Date: _____

World Map

Directions: Write the number for each ocean on the correct line on the map. Then, use different-color pencils or markers to color the oceans.

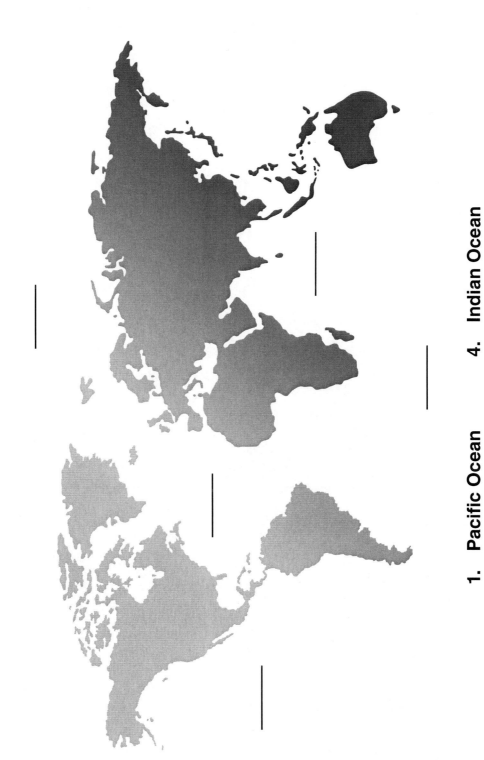

1. **Pacific Ocean**

2. **Arctic Ocean**

3. **Atlantic Ocean**

4. **Indian Ocean**

5. **Southern Ocean**

Tile Equations

Brain-Powered Strategy 🧑‍🤝‍🧑

Matchmaker

Standards

Recognize area as an attribute of plane figures and understand concepts of area measurement

Represents problems situations in a variety of forms

Vocabulary Words

- area
- diagram
- manipulatives
- numerical expression

Materials

- *Measuring Areas* (page 118)
- *Tile Equations* (page 119)
- *Tile Diagram Cards* (page 120)
- *Grid Paper* (page 121)
- transparency of *Grid Paper*
- address labels
- projector
- 12 one-inch transparent plastic tiles
- 12 one-inch tiles (one set for every two students)

Preparation Note: Prior to the lesson, write the numerical equations for the areas of each shape on the *Tile Diagram Cards* (page 120) on address labels (e.g., $2 \times 2 = 4$). Each set of five address labels should correspond to one set of *Tile Diagram Cards*.

Procedures

Model

1. Display a copy of the *Measuring Areas* activity sheet (page 118) to students. Have students estimate the area of the rectangle in inches. Ask students to brainstorm various ways to find the exact area of the rectangle.

2. Tell students that one way they could solve this problem is to use manipulatives. Demonstrate how to use one-inch transparent tiles to fill in the rectangle with four rows of three tiles.

3. Show students how to find the area of the rectangle by multiplying the number of tiles of the rectangle's length by the width. Demonstrate how to write the numerical equation $3 \times 4 = 12$.

Tile Equations *(cont.)*

Apply/Analyze

4. Assign each student a partner and give each pair a set of 12 one-inch tiles. Instruct students to practice making squares and rectangles with various dimensions.

5. Distribute copies of the *Tile Equations* activity sheet (page 119). Using the activity sheet, have them draw diagrams of one of their shapes and write the equation for the area of the shape.

6. Divide students into groups of five and distribute address labels with numerical equations on them *(2 × 6 = 12 sq. units, 2 × 2 = 4 sq. units, 2 × 3 = 6 sq. units, 3 × 3 = 9 sq. units, 1 × 8 = 8 sq. units)*. Explain the instructions for the activity, and show students how to match the diagram on the *Tile Diagram Cards* (page 120) with the numerical expression on the address label. You may wish to use larger versions of the cards found on the Digital Resource CD (filename: Enlarged Cards—tilediagramcards.pdf). Explain the *Matchmaker* strategy to students. (For detailed information on this strategy, see page 17.)

7. Guide students through the first round of the activity. After completing the round, have students mix up the cards and return them to the center of the circle. Instruct students to switch address labels and play again.

Evaluate/Create

8. Tell students that they will now have chances to use the skills they just learned to design a floor plan for a house. Distribute the *Grid Paper* activity sheet (page 121) to students, and display a copy of the grid paper on the projector. Demonstrate how to draw a series of connected squares and rectangles to represent the rooms in a house. Remind students that all rooms need to be either squares or rectangles.

9. Explain to students that they will also need to calculate the area for each room. Demonstrate how to determine the length and width of each room and write the numerical equation to figure out the area. Then, have them add up the areas of each room to determine the area of the entire floor plan.

10. Give students time to share their floor plans with their peers. If time permits, show them how to use symbols to indicate features such as doors and windows on their floor plans.

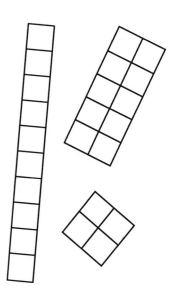

Name: _____   Date: _____

Measuring Areas

Directions: Fill the rectangle with one-inch tiles. Count the total number of tiles to get the area, and write the number in the space below. Count the length and width of the rectangle. Use these numbers to write a numerical expression showing the area of the rectangle.

Area = _____

Numerical Expression

length × width = _____ × _____ = _____

Name: _____ Date: _____

Tile Equations

· ·

Directions: Make a square or a rectangle with your tiles. Draw a diagram of your shape. Label the length and width of the shape. Use these numbers to write a numerical expression showing the area of the shape.

Diagram

```
┌─────────────────────────────────────────┐
│                                           │
│                                           │
│                                           │
│                                           │
│                                           │
│                                           │
│                                           │
│                                           │
│                                           │
│                                           │
│                                           │
│                                           │
│                                           │
│                                           │
│                                           │
└─────────────────────────────────────────┘
```

Numerical Expression

_____

Tile Diagram Cards

Teacher Directions: Copy and cut apart the cards below. Make enough sets so that there is a set for each group of five students.

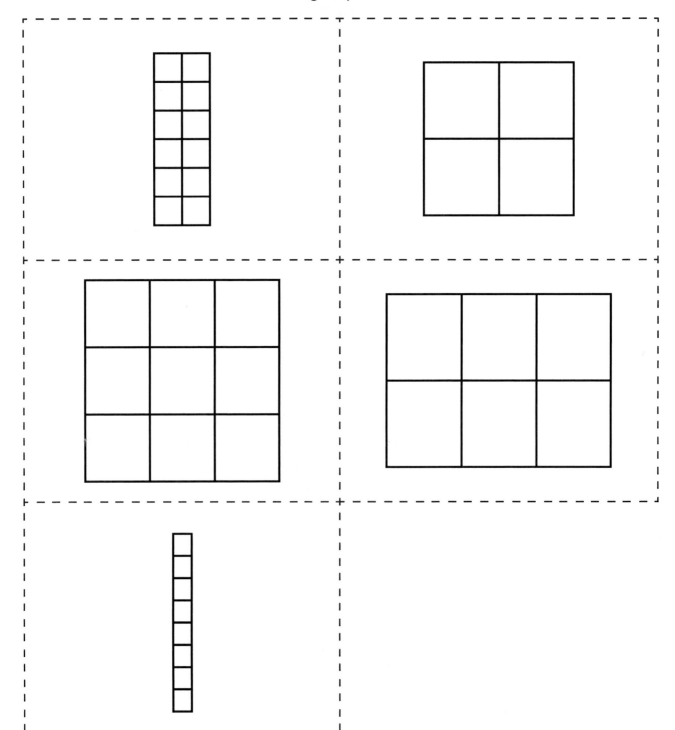

Name: _____ Date: _____

Grid Paper

Directions: Draw your floor plan using the grid below. Each room must be either a square or rectangle. The length and width of each room should not exceed 10 units.

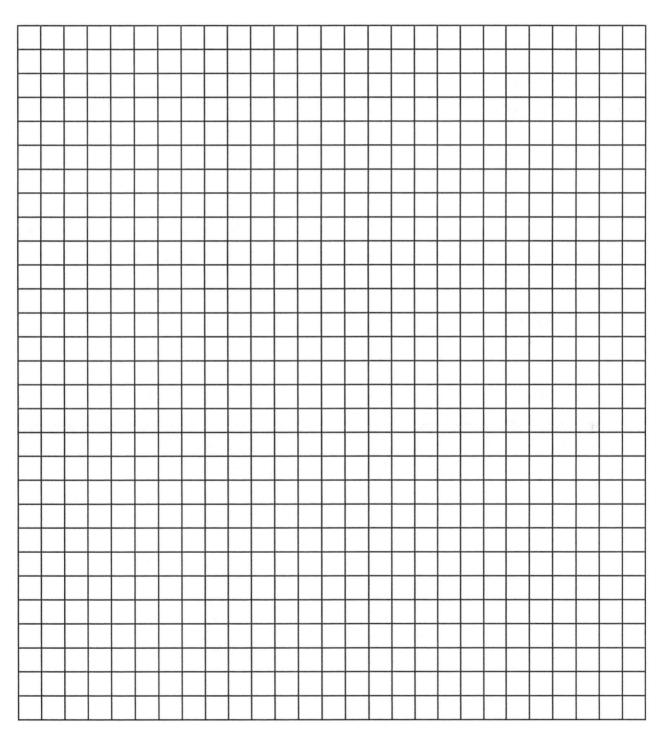

Concluding Statements

Brain-Powered Strategy	**Standards**
Just Say It	Write informative/explanatory texts to examine a topic and convey ideas and information clearly Provide a concluding statement or section

Vocabulary Words

- concluding statement
- paragraph structure
- summarize

Materials

- *Paragraph Organizer* (page 124)
- *Complete the Paragraph* (page 125)
- *Just Say It Notes* (page 126)
- timer
- background materials on chosen topic

Preparation Note: Prior to the lesson, choose a topic of recent study from a science or social studies unit. Give students time to review their notes, discuss the topic with a partner, or read additional information on the topic as a way to activate their prior knowledge about the subject matter.

Procedures

Model

1. Distribute copies of the *Paragraph Organizer* activity sheet (page 124) to students. Write an opening sentence about the chosen topic on the activity sheet, and display it for students. Tell students that you need their help to complete the paragraph.

2. Have the class work together to brainstorm three important facts that they want to include in the body of the paragraph.

3. Discuss the role of a concluding statement in a paragraph. Ask each student to write down his or her own concluding statement for the paragraph on his or her sheet, and then call on some students to share their sentences aloud. Discuss the merits of each sentence, and then write your own summary sentence in the displayed *Paragraph Organizer* activity sheet.

4. Review the paragraph structure on the *Paragraph Organizer* activity sheet, and discuss how this type of structure facilitates reading and comprehension.

Concluding Statements *(cont.)*

Apply/Analyze

5. Assign each student a partner, and have the pairs sit facing each other at their desks. Distribute a copy of the *Complete the Paragraph* activity sheet (page 125) to each student, and have them read the paragraph.

6. Explain the *Just Say It* strategy to students. (For detailed information on this strategy, see page 18.) Help students identify themselves as either Partner *A* or Partner *B*. Distribute copies of the *Just Say It Notes* activity sheet (page 126) to students. Set a timer for 30 seconds, and ask all of the Partner *A*s in the class to share their thoughts about the paragraph while all of the Partner *B*s listen. Then, provide time for the Partner *B*s to respond. All Partner *A*s should take notes on the feedback on the *Just Say It Notes* activity sheet. Switch roles and repeat the exercise.

7. Once both partners have had a chance to discuss and give feedback, instruct students to review their notes from the *Just Say It Notes* activity sheet, think about how they plan to solve the problem, and then write a concluding statement for the paragraph on the *Complete the Paragraph* activity sheet.

Evaluate/Create

8. Have students write their own paragraphs about the chosen topic from Step 1. Advise students to write informational paragraphs using their knowledge about the subject.

9. Repeat the *Just Say It* strategy, using the student-written paragraphs and new *Just Say It Notes* activity sheets.

10. When both students have shared their paragraphs and received feedback from their partners, give students time to revise their paragraphs and incorporate the feedback.

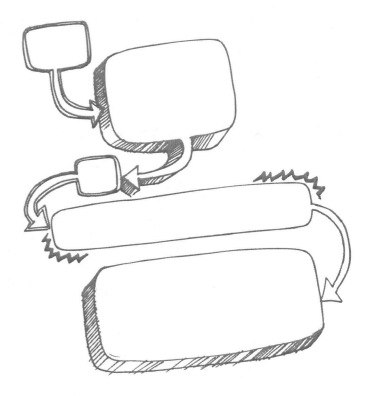

Name: _____   Date: _____

Paragraph Organizer

∙∙∙

Directions: Use the sections below to demonstrate how to organize a paragraph.

Opening Sentence

Supporting Details

Concluding Statement

Name: _____ Date: _____

Complete the Paragraph

Directions: Read the paragraph below. After completing the *Just Say It Notes* activity sheet, use your notes to write a concluding sentence for the paragraph on the lines below.

Cacti have many adaptations that make it possible for them to live in hot and dry desert climates. Because it rains very infrequently in the desert, many desert plants have the ability to store water in their stems and leaves. Some desert plants have no leaves at all and instead conduct photosynthesis in their stems. This absence of leaves prevents water loss during the process of photosynthesis. Desert plants also grow very slowly, thus requiring less energy, and they have extensive root systems that go deep into the ground or cover a wide area in order to absorb water.

_____

_____

_____

_____

_____

_____

_____

_____

Name: _____ Date: _____

Just Say It Notes

Directions: After sharing your thoughts with your partner, record the feedback your partner gives you in the space below. Then, at the bottom of the page write how you can use this feedback to improve your comprehension.

Notes on Feedback

_____

_____

_____

_____

_____

Plans to Incorporate the Feedback

_____

_____

_____

_____

Wise Word Problems

Brain-Powered Strategy	**Standard**
Just Say It	Use multiplication and division within 100 to solve word problems in situations involving equal groups, arrays, and measurement quantities

Vocabulary Words

- equal groups
- numerical equation
- variable
- word problem

Materials

- *Just Say It Word Problem* (page 129)
- *Just Say It Notes* (page 126)
- *My Word Problem* (page 130)
- large clear jar filled with pretzels or other small objects
- timer
- index cards

Preparation Note: Prior to the lesson, select an item (something you can later distribute to students), count out a number that is evenly divisible by the number of students in class, and place all of the objects in a clear jar. In this lesson, we will use pretzels as an example, but any small object may be substituted.

Procedures

Model

1. Display the jar containing the pretzels. Write the following question on the board: *If there are 52 pretzels in the jar and 26 students in the class, how many pretzels will each student get if the pretzels are divided into equal groups?* (Substitute the correct numbers depending on your number of students.)

2. Ask students to suggest ways to solve the word problem. Record their ideas on the board. Explain the various methods of solving word problems, and tell students that you will be using both drawings and numerical equations to solve this problem.

3. Demonstrate on the board how to draw a picture to solve the problem. Discuss other ways to illustrate the problem.

4. Think aloud as you translate the drawing into a numerical equation. Explain how you used the variable *x* to represent the number of pretzels in each group. Write each step as you work through the problem to find the answer.

Wise Word Problems *(cont.)*

Apply/Analyze

5. Divide students into pairs, and have them sit facing their partners at desks. Distribute copies of the *Just Say It Word Problem* activity sheet (page 129) to students and ask them to read the problem quietly to themselves.

6. Explain the *Just Say It* strategy to students. (For detailed information on this strategy, see page 18.) Assign each student a role as either Partner *A* or Partner *B*. Distribute copies of the *Just Say It Notes* activity sheet (page 126) to students. Set a timer for 30 seconds, and ask all of the Partner *A*s in the class to share their thoughts about the word problem while all of the Partner *B*s listen. Then, provide time for the Partner *B*s to respond. All Partner *A*s should take notes on their partner's feedback using the *Just Say It Notes* sheet. Switch roles and repeat the exercise.

7. Instruct students to review their notes from the *Just Say It Notes* activity sheet, and think about how they plan to solve the problem. Have students draw a picture illustrating the word problem and write a numerical equation representing the problem on their activity sheet. Once they have completed these steps, ask them to find the answer to the problem.

8. Discuss students' drawings, equations, and answers as a class and allow students to correct their work, as necessary.

Evaluate/Create

9. Distribute the *My Word Problem* activity sheet (page 130) to students. Have each student write his or her own word problem on the activity sheet. Tell students that all of the quantities in the word problem should not exceed 100 and that the problem should be able to be solved using whole numbers. In the designated space on the activity sheet, ask each student to draw a picture illustrating the problem, write a numerical equation, and find the answer to his or her own word problem.

10. Repeat the *Just Say It* strategy using the student-written word problems and new *Just Say It Notes* activity sheets. Each student should read his or her own word problem and explain the work on his or her activity sheet to a partner.

11. When both students have shared their work and received feedback from their partners, give students time to revise their word problems by incorporating their partners' feedback and correcting any mistakes.

12. Have students write their revised word problems on index cards and switch cards with a new partner. Give students time to solve the problem and discuss the solution with the student who wrote the problem.

Name: _____ Date: _____

Just Say It Word Problem

Directions: Read the word problem below. After completing the *Just Say It* activity with your partner, create a drawing that illustrates the word problem in the appropriate box below. Then, write a numerical expression representing the problem, and write the solution to the problem at the bottom.

Word Problem
Right now, your brother can type 12 words per minute on the computer. How long will it take him to type 60 words?

Drawing

Numerical Expression

Solution

Name: _____   Date: _____

My Word Problem

. . . .

Directions: Write your own word problem in the space below. Create a drawing that illustrates the word problem, and then write a numerical equation representing the problem in the appropriate boxes. Write the solution to the problem at the bottom of the page.

Word Problem

Drawing

Numerical Expression

Solution

Repel or Attract?

Brain-Powered Strategy	**Standard**
Just Say It	Knows that magnets attract and repel each other and attract certain kinds of other materials

Vocabulary Words

- attract
- magnet
- repel

Materials

- *Magnetic Predictions* (page 133)
- *Just Say It Notes* (page 126)
- paper clip
- fishing line
- tape
- timer
- set of magnets that both attract and repel
- sets of six metal items and other objects

Preparation Note: Prior to the lesson, attach a paper clip to a piece of fishing line and tape the other end of the fishing line to a desk at the front of the classroom. Wrap one of the magnets in a sheet of paper.

Procedures

Model

1. To arouse students' curiosity, have them gather around the desk at the front of the classroom and ask if they think it is possible to make the paper clip float without touching it. Using a magnet wrapped in paper, make the paper clip float up into the air.

2. Gather students' prior knowledge about magnets by creating a word web on the board at the front of the classroom.

3. Ask students if all magnets will stick to one another. Demonstrate the forces of attraction and repulsion using magnets.

4. Discuss the practical applications of magnets (e.g., sticking papers to refrigerators, deciphering direction with a compass). Ask students if magnets are attracted to things besides other magnets.

Repel or Attract? *(cont.)*

Apply/Analyze

5. Distribute copies of the *Magnetic Predictions* activity sheet (page 133) to students. Assign each student a partner, and give each pair a tray with various objects. Have students divide the objects into a group of objects that they think will stick to a magnet and a group of objects that they think will not stick. Ask students to record their predictions and their reasoning on their *Magnetic Predictions* activity sheet.

6. Give each pair of students a magnet and have them test each object to determine whether it is magnetic. Ask them to record the results of their experiments on the right side of the *Magnetic Predictions* activity sheet.

7. Arrange the pairs so that they are facing their partners at their desks. Explain the *Just Say It* strategy to students. (For detailed information on this strategy, see page 18.) Assign each student a role as either Partner *A* or Partner *B*.

8. Explain that you want them to consider the results of their experiments and discuss their new knowledge and questions about magnets. Distribute copies of the *Just Say It Notes* activity sheet (page 126) to students. Set a timer for 30 seconds, and ask all of the Partner *A*s in the class to share their thoughts about magnets while all of the Partner *B*s listen. Then, provide time for the Partner *B*s to respond. All Partner *A*s should take notes on their partner's feedback, using the *Just Say It Notes* activity sheet. Switch roles, and repeat the exercise.

Evaluate/Create

9. Instruct students to review their notes on the *Just Say It Notes* activity sheet. Have students write paragraphs summarizing their learning about magnets.

10. Repeat the *Just Say It* strategy with new partners using the student-written paragraphs about magnets and the new *Just Say It Notes* activity sheets. Each student should read his or her own paragraph and then take notes on the feedback from his or her partner.

11. When both students have shared their work and received feedback from their partners, encourage students to incorporate the feedback into their paragraphs and write revised versions.

Name: _____ Date: _____

Magnetic Predictions

Directions: List the objects on your tray in the left column. With your partner, sort the objects into two groups depending on whether you think they will be magnetic. Then, record your predictions and your findings.

Object	Prediction: Magnetic? Yes/No	Test: Magnetic? Yes/No

Tell Me a Story

Brain-Powered Strategy	Standard
Reverse, Reverse!	Write narratives to develop real or imagined experiences or events using effective technique, descriptive details, and clear event sequences

Vocabulary Words

- characters
- details
- event sequence
- narrative

Materials

- *Story Diagram* (page 136)
- *Story Feedback* (page 137)
- narrative stories

Preparation Note: Prior to the lesson, read and discuss several narrative stories to activate students' prior knowledge about narrative literature.

Procedures

Model

1. Tell students that the class will work together to create a narrative.

2. Display the *Story Diagram* activity sheet (page 136) for students to see. Review the major features of a narrative listed on the diagram, and discuss the order in which these elements are generally introduced in order to allow the narrative to develop in a logical way.

3. Provide students with a starting point for the story (e.g., a character, a problem), and write it on the diagram. Have students help you fill in the rest of the diagram as they work together to create a story.

4. Using the *Story Diagram* activity sheet as a guide, have each student tell one element of the story aloud in chronological order until the entire story has been retold.

Tell Me a Story *(cont.)*

Apply/Analyze

5. Have students sit or stand in a circle. Explain how to use the strategy *Reverse, Reverse!* (For detailed information on this strategy, see page 19.)

6. Choose a student to be the judge and have him or her sit outside the circle. Instruct the judge to halt the game if at any point the narrative stops making sense or the sequence of events becomes illogical.

7. Tell students that they will go around the circle telling an imaginary story. Each student should add one detail or plot element when it is his or her turn. If students pause for more than five seconds, cannot come up with something to add to the story, or end the story before the allotted time, then the game reverses and continues in the opposite direction. Provide students with a designated amount of time for each round, and monitor them as they play.

Evaluate/Create

8. After students finish playing, have them go back to their desks and review the story they created. Distribute copies of the *Story Diagram* activity sheet to students, and help them fill in the elements of the story. Discuss any elements that were left out.

9. Assign each student a partner and have them evaluate the story created during the game. Ask them to discuss the following questions:

- Do you think the story was successful? Why or why not?

- Did the story develop in a logical manner?

- Did the story include the necessary literary elements (e.g., characters, setting)?

- What could be done to improve the story?

10. Have students develop and write their own narratives (real or imaginary). When they are finished, have them trade their stories with partners. Distribute copies of the *Story Feedback* activity sheet (page 137) to students. Ask them to provide feedback on their partners' stories using the *Story Feedback* activity sheet.

11. Give students the opportunity to revise, edit, and publish their narratives.

Name: _____ Date: _____

Story Diagram

Directions: Fill in the story elements in the diagram below.

Characters

Setting

Describe the problem(s):

Sequence of events:

Name: _____ Date: _____

Story Feedback

Directions: Read your partner's story. Answer the questions below, and give the form back to your partner.

1. Do you think the story developed in a logical manner? Why or why not?

   _____

   _____

   _____

2. Did the story contain characters, a setting, and a sequence of events? List the characters, setting, and key events from the story.

   _____

   _____

   _____

3. What could be added or changed to improve the story?

   _____

   _____

   _____

4. What did you like best about the story?

   _____

   _____

   _____

History Buff

Brain-Powered Strategy	Standard
Reverse, Reverse!	Knows the chronological order of major historical events that are part of the state's history

Vocabulary Words

- chronological order
- historical event
- sequence
- timeline

Materials

- *Historical Event Facts* (page 140)
- *List of Historical Events* (page 141)
- *Timeline* (page 142)
- *Book Template* (page 143)
- *Cover Page Template* (page 144)
- research materials for gathering information on historical events (e.g., encyclopedias, books)
- slips of paper
- bowl
- sticky notes
- glue or tape
- construction paper
- markers or colored pencils
- stapler

Preparation Note: Prior to this lesson, select a series of historical events from your state's history (one event for every two students), and collect research materials for the students to use to learn about the events. Write the name of each event on a slip of folded paper, and put all of the events into a bowl. Additionally, write the names of these events on the *List of Historical Events* activity sheet (page 141).

Procedures

Model

1. Assign each student a partner, and have one student from each pair draw the name of an event out of the bowl.

2. Distribute copies of the *Historical Event Facts* activity sheet (page 140) to students. Using research materials or the Internet, instruct students to collect the basic facts about their chosen event, using the *Historical Event Facts* activity sheet.

History Buff *(cont.)*

3. Create a timeline on the board. Have each pair of students come to the front of the room and briefly tell the class about the event they researched. Then, have them place a sticky note with the name of their event on the timeline.

4. Distribute a *List of Historical Events* activity sheet and a *Timeline* activity sheet (pages 141–142) to each student. Instruct students to cut apart the two timeline sections and glue or tape them together to create one large timeline. Then, have them glue the complete timeline onto construction paper.

5. Using the timeline at the front of the class as a guide, have students cut out the events from the *List of Historical Events* activity sheet, and glue them to the construction paper in the appropriate section of the timeline.

Apply/Analyze

6. Remove an event from the timeline, and hold it in front of you. Go around the room, calling on one pair of students at a time. When you call on a pair, those students must say *before* or *after* according to whether the event they researched occurred before or after the event you selected from the timeline. Encourage them to respond as quickly as possible.

7. Have students sit or stand in a circle. Explain how to use the strategy *Reverse, Reverse!* (For detailed information on this strategy, see page 19.)

8. Choose a student to be the judge, and have him or her sit outside the circle. Instruct the judge to halt the game and reverse the direction if at any point the students say an event that does not adhere to the stated rule (e.g., name an event that occurs after _____) or is not in chronological order.

9. For an easier version of the game, state a "before" or "after" rule at the beginning of the game, such as, "Events that occurred before _____ (date or event)" and allow students to use their timelines as a reference. For a more challenging game, do not state a rule and have students list historical events in chronological order without using their timelines.

Evaluate/Create

10. After students finish playing *Reverse, Reverse!*, have them go back to their desks and select six events that they would like to include in a book.

11. Give each student six book pages—three copies of the *Book Template* (page 143) cut in half, plus one *Cover Page Template* (page 144). On each page, have the student write the name of the event and the date. Then, have students create an illustration depicting the event. If there is additional time, have them illustrate the cover page using markers or colored pencils.

12. Instruct students to arrange their book pages so the events are in chronological order. Help students staple them together.

13. Give students an opportunity to share their books with a partner or in a small group.

Name: _____ Date: _____

Historical Event Facts

· ·

Directions: Use the boxes below to record important information about your historical event.

Name of Event:	**Date:**

What occurred?

Where did it occur?

Who was there?

Why was it significant?

Name: _____ Date: _____

List of Historical Events

Directions: Cut the boxes apart, and glue the historical events to your timeline in chronological order.

Name: _____   Date: _____

Timeline

. . . .

Directions: Glue each historical event onto the timeline in chronological order. Write the date the event occurred underneath the name of the event. Use both above and below the timeline. If necessary, draw a line from the event to the timeline to show where it belongs.

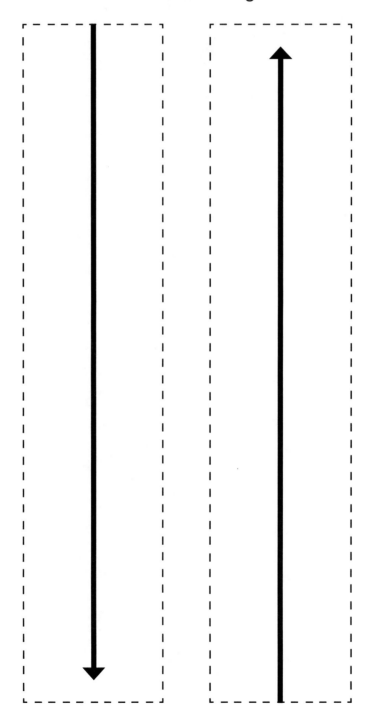

Book Template

Teacher Directions: Make three copies per student and cut apart to create six-page books.

Event:

Date:

Event:

Date:

Cover Page Template

Teacher Directions: Have students color or decorate their cover pages. Then, cut them out and staple them to the fronts of their books.

My State Historical Events
By:

_____

My State Historical Events
By:

_____

Prove It!

Brain-Powered Strategy	Standard
Reverse, Reverse!	Ask and answer questions to demonstrate understanding of a text, referring explicitly to the text as the basis for the answers

Vocabulary Words

- citation
- quotation
- source
- text-dependent question

Materials

- *Prove It!* (page 147)
- informational article on a chosen topic
- index cards
- bowl
- additional text on the same informational topic
- poster board
- tape

Preparation Note: Prior to the lesson, decide on an informational topic that students will study through the use of the *Reverse, Reverse!* strategy. The topic of fossils will be used as an example in this lesson.

Procedures

Model

1. Distribute a copy of the informational article or text on the topic (e.g., fossils) to each student. Have them read the article and highlight or take notes on important points or questions.

2. Discuss the text as a class. Take notes on the board to summarize the new information in the text.

3. Distribute two index cards to students. Have them write a question derived from the text on one card and the answer, including a quotation from the text and the location, on the other card.

4. Instruct students to keep the card with the answer and put their card containing the question in a bowl. Distribute copies of the *Prove It!* activity sheet (page 147) to students. Randomly distribute the questions, one to each student, and instruct students to use the *Prove It!* activity sheet to record the question, answer, and location of the information.

5. Divide students into small groups, and have them share their questions and answers with their classmates.

Prove It! *(cont.)*

Apply/Analyze

6. Have students sit or stand in a circle. Explain the strategy *Reverse, Reverse!* to students. (For detailed information on this strategy, see page 19).

7. Choose a student to be the judge, and have him or her sit outside the circle. Instruct the judge to halt the game and reverse the direction if at any point students say a fact that does not make sense or is untrue. When this occurs, the judge interrupts the game by saying, "Prove it!" and the student who said the fact must refer back to the text in order to provide evidence to support whatever he or she said.

8. To provide structure for the game, give students a subtopic, such as *plant fossils* or *animal fossils*, and play each round with a new subtopic to enhance learning.

Evaluate/Create

9. Tell students that they will work together to create a question-and-answer game to help them learn and review information about the topic. Provide students with another article or text containing additional information on the chosen topic. Have each student read the text either in class or for homework.

10. Give each student an index card and have them write a text-dependent question on one side and the answer, including a text citation, on the reverse.

11. Tape the top of each index card to a poster board, with the question side showing. It should be possible to flip the card over to read the answer on the back.

12. Divide the class into two teams. Take turns asking and answering questions from the poster board. Tally the number of points each team earns by providing the correct answer to determine a winner.

13. To add more complexity to the game, assign different points to different questions, depending on their difficulty. Invite another third-grade class studying the same topic to come and play the game with your class.

Name: _____ Date: _____

Prove It!

· ·

Directions: Record the question from your selected index card in the top box. Write your answer and the source of the information in the two following boxes. Be sure to include support from the text and a page number in your citation.

Question

Answer

Source

References Cited

Ainsworth, Larry. 2003. *Unwrapping the Standards: A Simple Process to Make Standards Manageable.* Englewood, CO: Lead+Learn Press.

Anderson, Lorin and David Krathwohl (Eds.). 2001. *Taxonomy for Learning, Teaching, and Assessing: A Revision of Bloom's Taxonomy of Educational Objectives.* Boston, MA: Pearson Education Group.

Baker, Linda. 2009. "Historical Roots of Inquiry in Metacognition." Retrieved from http://www.education.com/reference/article/metacognition.

Bloom, Benjamin (Ed.). 1956. *Taxonomy of Educational Objectives.* New York: David McKay Company.

Covington, Martin V. 2000. "Goal Theory, Motivation, and School Achievement: An Integrative Review." Retrieved from http://www2.csdm.qc.ca/SaintEmile/bernet/annexes/ASS6826/Covington2000.pdf.n 2000.

Csikszentmihalyi, Mihaly. 1996. *Creativity: Flow and the Psychology of Discovery and Invention.* New York: HarperCollins.

Doidge, Norman. 2007. *The Brain That Changes Itself: Stories of Personal Triumph from the Frontiers of Brain Science.* New York, NY: Penguin Books.

Flavell, John H. 1979. "Metacognition and Cognitive Monitoring: A New Area of Cognitive-Developmental Inquiry." *American Psychologist* 34: 906–911.

Harris, Bryan, and Cassandra Goldberg. 2012. *75 Quick and Easy Solutions to Common Classroom Disruptions.* Florence, KY: Routledge.

Huntington's Outreach Program for Education, at Stanford (HOPES). 2010. "Neuroplasticity." http://www.stanford.edu/group/hopes/cgi-bin/wordpress/2010/06/neuroplasticity.

Immordino-Yang, Mary H. and Matthias Faeth. 2010. "The Role of Emotion and Skilled Intuition in Learning." In *Mind, Brain, and Education: Neuroscience Implications for the Classroom*, edited by David A. Sousa, 69–83. Bloomington, IN: Solution Tree.

Jensen, Eric. 2005. *Teaching with the Brain in Mind.* Alexandria, VA: Association for Supervision and Curriculum Development.

McCombs, Barbara L. 1997. "Understanding the Keys to Motivation to Learn." Retrieved from http://incolor.inetnebr.com/fadams/motivation_exercise.htm.

Medina, John. 2008. *Brain Rules: 12 Principles for Surviving and Thriving at Work, Home, and School.* Seattle, WA: Pear Press.

Merzenich, Dr. Michael. 2013. *Soft-Wired: How the New Science of Brain Plasticity Can Change Your Life.* San Francisco, CA: Parnassus Publishing, LLC.

Overbaugh, Richard C. and Lynn Schultz. n.d. *Bloom's Taxonomy.* Retrieved from http://www.odu.edu/educ/roverbau/Bloom/blooms_taxonomy.htm.

References Cited *(cont.)*

Ratey, John J. 2008. *Spark: The Revolutionary New Science of Exercise and the Brain.* New York, NY: Little, Brown and Company.

Rock, David. 2009. *Your Brain at Work: Strategies for Overcoming Distraction, Regaining Focus, and Working Smarter All Day Long.* New York: Harper Collins.

Roth, LaVonna. 2012. *Brain-Powered Strategies to Engage All Learners.* Huntington Beach, CA: Shell Education.

Sousa, David A. 2006. *How the Brain Learns,* 3rd ed. Bloomington, IN: Solution Tree.

Thomas, Alice and Glenda Thorne. 2009. "How to Increase Higher Order Thinking." Retrieved from http://www.cdl.org/resourcelibrary/articles/HOT.php?type=subject&id=18.

Van Tassell, Gene. 2004 "Neural Pathway Development." Retrieved from http://www.brains.org/path.htm.

Vaynman, Shoshanna, Zhe Ying, and Fernando Gomez-Pinilla. "Hippocampal BDNF Mediates the Efficacy of Exercise on Synaptic Plasticity and Cognition." *European Journal of Neuroscience* 20 (2004): 2580–2590.

Webb, Norman L. "Alignment, Depth of Knowledge, and Change." Presented at the 50th annual meeting of the Florida Educational Research Association, Miami, FL. 2005. Abstract retrieved from http://facstaff.wcer.wisc.edu/normw/MIAMI%20FLORIDA%20 FINAL%20slides%2011-15-05.pdf.

Wiggins, Grant and Jay McTighe. *Understanding by Design (2nd ed.).* Upper Saddle River, NJ: Prentice Hall, 2005

Willis, Judy. *How Your Child Learns Best: Brain-Friendly Strategies You Can Use to Ignite Your Child's Learning and Increase School Success.* Naperville, IL: Sourcebooks, Inc., 2008.

Wyoming School Health and Physical Education. "Standards, Assessment, and Beyond." 2001. Retrieved May 25, 2006 from http://www.uwyo.edu/wyhpenet.

Contents of the Digital Resource CD

Pages	Lesson	Filename
29–34	Mapping Madness	mappingmadness.pdf
35–38; 34	Pizza Party!	pizzaparty.pdf
39–42; 34	Family Traits	familytraits.pdf
43–50	Getting to the Point (of View)	gettingtothepointofview.pdf
51–57	Data Displays	datadisplays.pdf
58–61; 55	Stars and Planets: Same or Different?	starsandplanets.pdf
62–67; 55	Mastering the Main Idea	masteringthemainidea.pdf
68–70	The Power of the Law	thepoweroftelaw.pdf
71–73	Water: A Case of Multiple Identities	water.pdf
74–76	Find Me a Reference	findmeareference.pdf
77–85	Map Experts	mapexperts.pdf
86–89	Mass Wizards	masswizards.pdf
90–93	Inquiry Tools	inquirytools.pdf
94–96	Event Sequencing	eventsequencing.pdf
97–98	Measurement Mania	measurementmania.pdf
99–100	Take a Stance	takeastance.pdf
101–108	Missing Links	missinglinks.pdf
109–115	Where Am I?	whereami.pdf
116–121	Tile Equations	tileequations.pdf
122–126	Concluding Statements	concludingstatements.pdf
127–130; 126	Wise Word Problems	wisewordproblems.pdf
131–133; 126	Repel or Attract?	repelorattract.pdf
134–137	Tell Me a Story	tellmeastory.pdf
138–144	History Buff	historybuff.pdf
145–147	Prove It!	proveit.pdf

Pages	Additional Resource	Filename/Folder Name
12–19	Overview of Strategies	overviewofstrategies.pdf
25–28	Standards	standards.pdf
NA	ABC Professor Notes Activity Sheet	abcnotes.pdf
N/A	Enlarged Activity Cards (This folder contains the following: linkingwordscards.pdf, oceanfacts.pdf, oceannames.pdf, tilediagramscards.pdf.)	Enlarged Cards

Notes

Notes